T0294240

CRICKET
IN
POETRY

CRICKET IN POETRY

Run-Stealers, Gatlings and Graces

BOB DORAN

First published by Pitch Publishing, 2024

Pitch Publishing
9 Donnington Park,
85 Birdham Road,
Chichester,
West Sussex,
PO20 7AJ
www.pitchpublishing.co.uk
info@pitchpublishing.co.uk

A CIP catalogue record is available for this book
from the British Library.

ISBN 978 1 80150 692 2

Typesetting and origination by Pitch Publishing
Printed and bound in India by Replika Press Pvt. Ltd.

CONTENTS

DEDICATION

My parents, Bob and Nellie Doran, were both born in Lancashire and lived in Walton-le-Dale, across the River Ribble from Preston. He was a cobbler and Preston North End supporter. She was a cotton worker. During the school holidays my mother once took me all the way to Old Trafford to watch Lancashire. It rained. Later, when I was playing for the village team, my father would come down the hill from his allotment to watch. They were not by any definition 'toffs' but in her later years my mother would still quote from a poem born on the cricket field of a public school in the south: 'Play up, play up, and play the game.'

PREFACE

by Mihir Bose

GEORGE BERNARD SHAW, writes Bob Doran, may have said the English not being a very spiritual people invented cricket to give themselves some idea of eternity, but I have always felt it was invented so that the English could be fiercely competitive and still claim the moral high ground, being morally right being of such importance to the English.

The very structure of cricket illustrates that wonderfully. Unlike almost all other sports, baseball apart, the two sets of players never take the field at the same time and do entirely opposite things on the field of play. In football both teams have 11 players on the field contesting the same ball. In cricket while 11 players gather on the field of play with a leather ball in their hands, they are faced with only two players from the opposition with a piece of wood in theirs. The fielders' objective is to make sure the batters are forced to leave the field of play and become spectators. And in order to do that in most cases they have to appeal to two umpires, normally dressed in white, who act as a sort of court of appeal on the field of play. If the fielders do not appeal the umpires will not give a batter out even if the batter is.

In football, appeals have nothing to do with the referee giving a penalty. In fact, players who appeal excessively could even be sent off. This need to appeal raises the question of whether the appeal is morally justified. When it is felt not to be it can produce high drama as it did during the 2023 Ashes Test at Lord's.

Then the Australian wicketkeeper Alex Carey, finding that Jonny Bairstow, the England batsman, was out of his crease, threw down the stumps and when the Australians appealed he was given out. Bairstow, thinking the ball was 'dead', i.e., not in play, had stepped out of his crease to do a bit of patting of the pitch, what cricketers rather grandly call 'gardening'. But the umpires had not called over which would have made the ball dead and had no option but to give Bairstow out. Under the laws of the game the Australians were entitled to appeal, but it was held to be not in the spirit of the game. The reaction produced a howl of protest with some calling the Australians cheats; even Prime Minister Rishi Sunak intervened to rebuke the Australians, and in the Long Room at Lord's such was the reaction of some MCC members towards the Australian players that MCC concluded that there had been 'abusive, offensive or inappropriate behaviour or language' by three members. One was expelled and two others suspended – one for four and a two and a half half years.

So, it is no surprise that the game lends itself to literature. But while much has been written on this subject what makes this book exceptional is that Doran uses the poetry the game has inspired to write a wonderfully concise and informative history of cricket. And unlike many English books on cricket, which even in our age are dreadfully English-centric, Doran has a wide-angled world view setting this book apart. He mentions that back on 18 August 1885, a 13-year-old schoolboy, A.E.J. Collins, who was born in India but schooled in this country, made 628 not out in a school match to set a record.

Many other books might have stopped there. But Doran mentions that the record was surpassed in January 2016 by a 15-year-old Indian schoolboy who was born and brought up in India and was not only different to Collins because of the colour of his skin but also his background. Pranav Dhanawade, the son of a rickshaw driver, scored 1,009 runs over two days in a school match.

I also love the way Doran uses poetry and the life of poets to provide wonderful history lessons that go beyond the game. We learn about the lives of Francis Thompson, who wrote *At Lord's* and Henry Newbolt, who wrote *Vitai Lampada*. They were born two years apart in industrial towns in Victorian England and were sons of prosperous and religious families. Doran rightly highlights that Newbolt's poetry often blended 'patriotism, militarism and a dim view of foreigners' and in *Vitai Lampada* he took liberties with facts to present the English in the best possible light.

Even more striking is how he links the cricket verses these Victorians produced with Lord Kitchener and Lord Beginner's 1950 *Victory Calypso*, celebrating the first West Indies Test win in England. It produced the immortal phrase 'Cricket, lovely Cricket' which has since come to symbolise West Indian cricket and the chorus 'With those two little pals of mine, Ramadhin and Valentine', the two spinners who mesmerised the English batsmen. Doran narrates how the calypso came to be written during the Lord's Test providing it in its entirely. It makes a lovely read as does this book.

For me the reference to Walter de la Mare, whose poetry was part of my Jesuit school upbringing, was particularly touching. I could have done with more about him but that may be for another book.

Mihir Bose,

London,

November 2023

INTRODUCTION

'SOME OF the great cricket prose is poetry.'

So wrote the New Zealand-born spin bowler, Clarrie Grimmett, who played in 37 Test matches for Australia. Grimmett played cricket (and golf) alongside another great Australian spinner, Arthur Mailey, some of whose prose fitted Grimmett's description.

As a boy, Mailey hero-worshipped the great Australian batsman Victor Trumper. Young Arthur never saw the legend bat, though he did spot him passing through the entry gate to Sydney Cricket Ground and once managed to sit opposite him on a train. A few years later, as a young man, he found himself down to play for his club, Redfern, against Paddington, the team of Victor Trumper.

In his book *10 for 66 and All That*, Mailey recounts how, after an anxious few days, Saturday came and he found himself brought on unnervingly early to bowl at his hero. His first few deliveries were shrugged to the boundary or nudged aside, so Mailey decided to try a 'Bosie' or 'wrong 'un'. Trumper leapt forward to attack but found the ball drifting away from him. He was stranded and the bails were whipped off. As he walked past Mailey on his way to the pavilion, he smiled, patted the back of his bat, and said, 'It was too good for me.' Mailey concludes, 'There was no triumph in me as I watched the receding figure. I felt like a boy who had killed a dove.'

This last line is cricket poetry as cricket prose, and it's hard to imagine it in any other sport, not Muhammad Ali on knocking out Sonny Liston in the first round, or John McEnroe on defeating Bjorn Borg (or vice versa).

George Bernard Shaw reportedly observed that the English were not a very spiritual people, so they invented cricket to give themselves some idea of eternity. (He did get his comeuppance. The American humorist, Will Rogers, suggested that Shaw's *Back to Methuselah* had the same feeling of endlessness as a Test match.) It may be cricket's gentle pace, the literary tastes of its early supporters and its rural beginnings leading to pastoral nostalgia, which give the game its timeless, contemplative quality. This in turn inspires its followers to produce a literature which, at its best, leaves the game itself far behind.

Other sports have their prose. Baseball has novels like W.P. Kinsella's *Field of Dreams*, Bernard Malamud's *The Natural*, and Philip Roth's modestly titled *The Great American Novel*. Football inspired Nick Hornby's *Fever Pitch*.

Rugby League has David Storey's *This Sporting Life*. But cricket has produced poetry unequalled since the Theban poet Pindar celebrated the achievements of ancient Olympians.

Not all cricket poetry is memorable. Some of it is funny or moving, some arch or dull. A fair proportion of writers can't resist rhyming cricket with wicket, though John Galsworthy avoids it in the White Monkey instalment of *The Forsyte Saga*.

An angry young husband called Bicket
Said 'Turn yourself round and I'll kick it;
You have painted my wife
In the nude to the life,
Do you think, Mr. Greene, it was cricket?

There's also a great deal of nostalgia for seasons and heroes past. As the composer and author Humphrey Clucas puts it,

Of course it's all

Decline and fall;

The Snows of yesteryear

Increase the thirst

For Rhodes and Hirst

And older, rarer beer.

So here's to Peel,

And Studd and Steel;

Turn off the TV Test,

And let the page

Improve with age,

Whatever was, was best.

Two poems stand out, Francis Thompson's *At Lord's* and Henry Newbolt's *Vitai Lampada*, though both go beyond the game itself. *Vitai Lampada* moves from cricket to war or, as Newbolt would see it, to chivalry. *At Lord's* echoes with age and sadness. The two poets were born two years apart, both in industrial towns in Victorian England. Both were sons of prosperous and religious families. But one became a drug addict and sometime rough sleeper, much of whose poetry is religious, but who was added to the list of Jack the Ripper suspects. The other, by contrast, was a pillar of society, a friend of literary greats and a confidant of prime ministers and governments.

But both produced cricket verses which have survived in a way unequalled until Lord Kitchener and Lord Beginner's 1950 *Victory Calypso*, celebrating the first West Indies Test win in England:

Cricket, lovely Cricket,
At Lord's where I saw it;
Cricket, lovely Cricket,
At Lord's where I saw it;
Yardley tried his best

But Goddard won the Test.

They gave the crowd plenty fun;

Second Test and West Indies won.

With those two little pals of mine

Ramadhin and Valentine.

A note to students of Latin, who may be wondering why it's *Vitai Lampada*, not Vitae. Newbolt lifted the phrase from *De Rerum Natura* by the Roman philosopher poet, Lucretius. His 'torch of life' was a reference to the ancient Olympic relay contest in which athletes passed on a torch and tried to reach the finish while it was still burning. Lucretius made it Vitai because he needed three syllables to fit his poem's dactylic hexameters.

AT LORD'S

It is little I repair to the matches of the
Southron folk,
Though my own red roses there may blow;
It is little I repair to the matches of the
Southron folk,
Though the red roses crest the caps, I know.
For the field is full of shades as I near a
shadowy coast,
And a ghostly batsman plays to the
bowling of a ghost,
And I look through my tears on a
soundless-clapping host
As the run stealers flicker to and fro,
To and fro:
O my Hornby and my Barlow long ago!

It's Glo'ster coming North, the irresistible,
The Shire of the Graces, long ago!

It's Gloucestershire up North, the irresistible,

And new-risen Lancashire the foe!

A Shire so young that has scarce

impressed its traces,

Ah, how shall it stand before all-

resistless Graces?

O, little red rose, their bats are as maces

To beat thee down, this summer long ago!

This day of seventy-eight they are come up

north against thee

This day of seventy-eight long ago!

The champion of the centuries, he cometh up

against thee,

With his brethren, everyone a famous foe!

The long-whiskered Doctor, that laugheth the

rules to scorn,

While the bowler, pitched against him, bans the

day he was born;

And G.F. with his science makes the fairest
    length forlorn;
They are come from the West to work thee woe!

It is little I repair to the matches of the
    Southron folk,
Though my own red roses there may blow;
It is little I repair to the matches of the
    Southron folk,
Though the red roses crest the caps, I know.
For the field is full of shades as I near a
    shadowy coast,
And a ghostly batsman plays to the
    bowling of a ghost,
And I look through my tears on a
    soundless-clapping host
As the run stealers flicker to and fro,
To and fro:
O my Hornby and my Barlow long ago!

VITAI LAMPADA

There's a breathless hush in the Close to-night –

Ten to make and the match to win –

A bumping pitch and a blinding light,

An hour to play and the last man in.

And it's not for the sake of a ribboned coat,

Or the selfish hope of a season's fame,

But his Captain's hand on his shoulder smote –

'Play up! play up! and play the game!'

The sand of the desert is sodden red, –

Red with the wreck of a square that broke; –

The Gatling's jammed and the Colonel dead,

And the regiment blind with dust and smoke.

The river of death has brimmed his banks,

And England's far, and Honour a name,

But the voice of a schoolboy rallies the ranks:

'Play up! play up! and play the game!'

This is the word that year by year,

While in her place the School is set,

Every one of her sons must hear,

And none that hears it dare forget.

This they all with a joyful mind

Bear through life like a torch in flame,

And falling fling to the host behind –

'Play up! play up! and play the game!'

Chapter 1

BOYS' TOWNS

IN ITS early centuries, cricket was a predominantly rural game, played mostly in the southern counties of England. But throughout the 1800s it was spreading across the country and moving into industrial towns in the Midlands and the North. These were the towns in which Francis Thompson and Henry Newbolt were born, a few years before the County Championship was formed.

Charles Dickens's *Hard Times* is a grim portrait of 19th-century industrial Britain. Published in 1854, it's set in Coketown, a place of filth, smells and misery. 'It had a black canal in it, and a river that ran purple with ill-smelling dye, and vast piles of buildings full of windows where there was a rattling and a trembling all day long, and where the piston of the steam-engine worked monotonously up and down like the head of an elephant in a state of melancholy madness.'

Coketown is Preston, once a small Lancashire market town, but by then a large industrial centre with cotton as its main product, thanks in part to the invention of the water frame by two local pioneers, Richard Arkwright and John Kay. By the 1850s much of the town was in the deepest squalor. A survey at the time reported, 'The site at the rear of the 17 houses on St Wilfred's Street contains 17 privies, 17 offal-ash pits, and 17 slop drains. These harbours for filth have soiled and choked the ground until they could be borne no longer.'

In October 1853, the cotton workers demanded that a cut in their pay made ten years previously should be restored. Some of the companies refused, the workers went on strike and the owners imposed a lock-out. The town generally supported the workers, and a weekly collection was started to support them.

On the last Saturday of January 1854, Dickens, a journalist by profession, had travelled to Preston to support the cotton workers and turned up unannounced at a union meeting in the Old Cock Pit, the former Temperance Hall, down Stoneygate. The following day he joined an open-air meeting with delegates from around the country, and on the Monday he was back at the Cock Pit to see piles of pennies given to those in need.

The North was well behind the South in the spread of cricket, but the game was well established in Preston by the time Francis Thompson was born. The Preston club was formed in 1820 and played on a number of pitches around the area including one at Penwortham Holme which the players reached by rowing up the River Ribble. Preston joined the Liverpool Competition in 1953. Until then it was all friendly matches, though, according to the club's history, some were less friendly than others. A row broke out in July 1833 when some of the Burnley players, who'd placed large bets on the result, tried to rig it by plying the Preston team with heavy liquor the night before.

Preston had been forewarned of the plot when an anonymous letter landed on the desk of the club secretary. It read, 'Mr Secretary, I was sojourning for the night in the town of Burnley when I chanced upon a party who, I ascertained, were about to play a match at cricket with your club. From the conversation that ensued I beg that no one at your club partake of any liquors offered to you on the eve of the match.' Preston ignored the warning and were in no fit state to play the following morning. To make matters worse their opening batsman Mr Kemp was hit on the ankle three times and could only run singles. Burnley won the match by 31 runs.

Not all Preston was Coketown. Winkley Street, a little turn off the main thoroughfare, Fishergate, leads to Winkley Square, a massive sunken park and garden built in the early 19th century.

The architectural critic, Ian Nairn, reckoned it was unlike anywhere else in Britain because it was not levelled out, but planted as it was and designed in the manner of federal-style squares in Boston and other American towns and cities.

Francis Thompson was born at 7 Winkley Street, probably on 16 December 1858. Probably, because while a bronze plaque on the house says the 16th, it shared the space for many years with a stone tablet saying the 18th. Thompson himself was even vaguer: 'I was born in 1858 or 1859. I never could remember and don't care which.'

He was the second-born son of Charles and Mary Thompson. Their first son had died after only a few days. Three sisters were to follow, Mary, Helen and Margaret, but Helen died of tuberculosis aged 15 months. After the repeal of anti-Catholic laws in the 18th century, Preston had become the leading Catholic town in the North West, and this may have drawn Charles and Mary. They were both converts to Roman Catholicism and Mary had been outlawed by her Anglican family because of it. Some of Charles's brothers were also converts and his two sisters became nuns. Charles practised medicine, first in Bristol, then as house-surgeon at a homeopathic dispensary in Manchester. His work in Preston was a mixture of medical and pastoral, much of it for poor people who could not afford to pay fees.

Francis was an unusual, distant child. By the age of seven he was deeply into the works of Shakespeare and Coleridge. He was to write later, 'There is a sense in which I have always been and even now remain a child. But in another sense I was never a child, never shared children's thoughts, ways, tastes, manner of life, and philosophy of life and outlook.'

Cricket was to become one of the great passions of his life, but for the young Thompson it was a solitary, not a team, game. He did play a little cricket with his sisters, reproducing the centuries of A.N. Hornby on the beach at Colwyn Bay, but apart from that his sisters remembered his solitary practice sessions in the garden, bowling a ball, running after it and bowling it again. This common kind of sibling cricket rivalry was echoed

half a century later by Hilaire Belloc, though the
ending may be less comfortable today:

I wish you'd speak to Mary, Nurse,
She's really getting worse and worse.
Just now when Tommy gave her out
She cried and then began to pout
And then she tried to take the ball
Although she cannot bowl at all.
And now she's standing on the pitch,
The miserable little Bitch!

The Thompson family eventually moved to
Winkley Square itself and in 1864 they decamped
to Ashton-under-Lyne, an industrial suburb of
Manchester. There was strong anti-Catholic
feeling there, and the family was confined to a
small circle of fellow Catholic friends, including
local priests. In May 1888, some 3,000 rioters
attacked Catholic homes, and the Thompson

family had to take refuge with others in a church. Like Winkley Street, the family home in Ashton was marked with a blue plaque. However, the building collapsed in 2014.

Bilston, north-west of Birmingham, was not Coketown, but in the 1860s it was just as gloomy and pungent. In fact, it was one of the most industrialised towns in England. Beneath it was the Ten Yard Seam of iron and the coal for the furnaces which smelted it. Henry Newbolt was to write of the streets where his nurse pushed his pram 'by black canals and among huge slag heaps where no grass could grow, where the sun rarely shone, where at night a man could read his newspaper by the glare of the blast furnaces'.

His father was the Reverend Henry Francis Newbolt, himself the son of Royal Navy captain Charles Newbolt. Charles had been a midshipman in Nelson's fleet and died young of yellow fever while commanding a merchant ship. His other son, also Charles, continued the family's nautical tradition as a merchant seaman.

Henry Francis was a churchman dedicated to the welfare of his flock, particularly the poorer ones. He began his church career as a curate in Maidstone, Kent where he met his first wife, Mary Jane Newham. She gave birth to a daughter, also Mary, but Mary Jane died at the age of 27. Henry Francis spent six years at St Matthew's, Walsall, and it was here that he met his second wife, Emily Stubbs. She was a teenager when they met. Her father was a wealthy businessman in the leather industry and her mother the daughter of a Jewish-Hungarian family of pencil-makers. Emily's father took against Henry Francis from the start, and when the couple were married on 5 December 1860 he stayed at home and left it to his wife to give their daughter away.

By now Henry Francis was established at the newly built church of St Mary's at Bilston.

Eighteen months after the wedding, Henry John was born on 6 June 1862. His brother Frank was born a year later, and their sister, Milly, two years after that.

Henry Francis's health had been poorer for some time and it now deteriorated. He was diagnosed with prostate and bladder ailments, and it seems likely that he had prostate cancer. He and his wife tried to escape the atmosphere of Bilston by spending six months at the rural vicarage of Coalbrookdale in Shropshire. He wrote to his son, 'Papa went for a walk today to Portobello where the young men were playing cricket – I wonder whether Harry will be fond of cricket?'

Henry Francis and Emily eventually decided to move back to Walsall, staying at Doveridge Close at the top of the town near St Matthew's Church. He died on 24 May 1866 while resting at Ilfracombe in Devon, aged 42. His father-in-law did not join the mourners at the funeral, but a crowd of poor people from Bilston walked to Walsall to pay their respects. At Bilston Church a tablet reads: 'His sun has gone down while it is still day.'

The family stayed at Doveridge Close, and every year Harry went with his mother to visit his father's grave in St Michael's Churchyard. Emily was stricken with grief for two years, and the children lived apart from her for much of the day, though she usually had tea with them and read to them. She did take the seven-year-old Harry to see Nelson's *Victory*, and a cousin, Captain Roberts, showed them round the ship. He took them to the cockpit, grabbed Harry, and made him lie flat on the spot where Nelson died. Harry treasured the memory.

Another family bereavement was to follow soon. Harry's older stepsister, Mary, had been sent to a finishing school in Germany. The school was tough, but Mary was strong-willed and would not be pushed around. She remained deeply fond of her brothers and sister back home. At the age of 17 she developed symptoms of consumption which gradually deteriorated. He mother panicked and two female friends were sent to bring her home. They boarded a boat, spending the first night in a public saloon until a couple of ladies offered Mary their private cabin. But she soon lost consciousness and died while still at sea, on 28 May 1870, aged 17 years and ten months.

Harry's early education was at home and somewhat erratic. But at the age of ten he was sent to the local St Mary's grammar school. The headmaster was a notorious flogger, but Harry was lucky to be taken in by the school's second master who taught him Latin, English and maths, plus a little Greek. He was then sent to a small preparatory school at Caistor on the Lincolnshire

Wold, in the hope that he would learn enough Latin to get him into Eton. In the event, he was sent to Clifton College near Bristol, with which the Caistor head had connections, and began his studies there in 1876.

Chapter 2

CHAMPION COUNTIES

WHILE FRANCIS and Harry were growing up, county cricket was coming of age with Lancashire and the rest of the northern half of England starting well behind the areas further south. The precise period in which the game was born is unclear and disputed, but by the early 1600s it was being played in villages across the southern counties.

Progress was more difficult in areas where the Puritans held sway and cricketing villagers were rebuked for playing such a frivolous game, especially on the Sabbath.

This religious zeal was still causing havoc two centuries later. John Major's account of cricket's early days, *More Than a Game*, recounts that, in 1843, seven boys from Hurley in Berkshire were fined three shillings plus 12 shillings costs for playing on the village green on the Sabbath. This caused an uproar, and the matter was raised in the House of Commons by Lord John Manners, 7th Earl of Rutland, Tory MP for Newark and a member of Benjamin Disraeli's Young England movement. He demanded to know of the Attorney General, 'If it was against the law for the working classes to play cricket on a Sunday, was it legal for the rich to ride in their carriages on the same day?' The answer was that it was lawful for the boys to play in their own parish but illegal to play in another one. In the end the boys' fines were paid by a private donor.

But the issue rumbled on. In 1858 a court at East Burnham in Buckinghamshire imposed fines of 15 shillings, or six weeks in Aylesbury jail for non-payment. In June 1885, there were clashes in Leicester between rival groups for and against cricket on the Sabbath. The anti crowd stormed the pitch and threatened to throw the players into the river. In the end they only threw the ball in. A cricket supporter's dog retrieved it, but the game was abandoned.

By the early 1700s the game was spreading into London and its suburbs. The drivers were members of the aristocracy, including some royals, and at the heart of it was gambling. Rich men organised matches with various numbers of friends and servants, usually agreeing on a prize for the winners. In 1751, the Earl of March and the Earl of Sandwich organised three matches for the prize of a thousand guineas, worth around £100,000 in 2024.

The money may have been behind some of the nastier incidents on and off the pitch. John

Major relates an incident in 1776 at a match between men from Kent and Essex at Tilbury. A row erupted over the eligibility of one of the Kent players and the Essex team refused to play. A fight broke out and one of the Kent men was shot and killed by an Essex player. In the violence that followed, an old man was stabbed with a bayonet and a soldier was shot dead. The Essex men fled, and the Kent team escaped in boats.

The earliest recorded team games were in villages in Kent, Surrey and Sussex, but through the 1700s the game was spreading south and west to Hampshire, Dorset, Gloucestershire, Somerset and Devon. By the 1780s matches were being played in Wales, by the gentry at Caernarvon, and in Scotland, at the estate of the Duke of Hamilton. But in much of northern England and the Midlands, including Lancashire, Cheshire, Cumberland, Westmoreland, Herefordshire,

Worcestershire and Staffordshire, hardly any cricket is recorded over the century.

During the same period, there were plenty of games involving county teams, but they were very different from the County Championship sides of a century later. Some local teams claimed to represent their whole county – Slindon represented Sussex, Dartford called itself Kent, and Hambledon was Hampshire. Other local clubs just borrowed the county name for the day.

The birth of genuine county clubs came in the middle of the 19th century. Over two decades, from 1839–59, four county teams were formed: Sussex in 1839, Nottinghamshire in 1841, Surrey in 1845 and Kent in 1859. More were to follow – Yorkshire and Hampshire in 1863, Middlesex and Lancashire in 1864, Worcestershire in 1865, Derbyshire in 1870, Gloucestershire in 1871, Somerset in 1875, Essex in 1876, and Leicestershire in 1879. Warwickshire joined the list in 1882. Northamptonshire formed in 1820 but did not join the Championship until 1905. The Glamorgan club was founded in 1888 but did not join the official list until 1921. Seven decades later Durham joined in 1992.

In the 1700s and early 1800s, counties could claim to be the champion team, but with no authority. Things became more formal in 1864 when newspapers and others began to agree a champion side each season. The contributors included the *Wisden Cricketers' Almanack*, John Lillywhite's publications, and W.G. Grace himself. To complicate matters, teams could decide which other counties they wanted to play against and which they did not, hence Lancashire's long wait for Gloucestershire to head north. Relatively few games were played and as late as 1880 there were only 46 fixtures. This undermined one of the principles of champion selection, that the team with fewest defeats topped the league. For example, in 1874 Derbyshire supporters claimed the title but their team had played only four matches while Yorkshire had played 12.

Throughout this period there were tensions between the North and Midlands and the South, partly because of differences between amateurs and professionals. Most county teams were captained by amateurs. By contrast, Nottinghamshire had five captains in the half-century from 1838. All five were professionals. The establishment view was put succinctly by Lord Hawke, who skippered Yorkshire and England over three decades from the 1880s, 'Pray God no professional shall ever captain England.'

The game became more formalised in 1873 when new rules came in to decide which team a player could represent. Up till then, players had been free to play for more than one county in the same season. Under the new rules all players, amateur or professional, had to choose before the opening of the season between the county in which they were born and the one in which they had been living for two years. A cricketer could also play for the county containing the family home, provided it remained open for him as an occasional resident.

The decisive step towards the modern Championship came late in 1889. On 10 December, county club secretaries met at Lord's for their AGM to agree a fixtures schedule for the following season. While they were making their plans, representatives of the leading eight counties from Gloucestershire, Kent, Lancashire, Middlesex, Nottinghamshire, Surrey, Sussex and Yorkshire held a private meeting to discuss the future of the Championship, and how to decide the champions.

By a majority they voted that the title should be decided on wins and losses only, with no reference to draws. The eight minor counties

– Derbyshire, Durham, Essex, Hampshire, Leicestershire, Somerset. Staffordshire and Warwickshire – held a meeting of their own and adopted the same rules. The first official County Championship match between Gloucestershire and Yorkshire began at Bristol on 12 May 1890. Yorkshire won by eight wickets, despite a century by Gloucestershire's James Cranston, the first in Championship history.

The rivalry of the Roses, Lancashire and Yorkshire, was now underway, but Francis Thompson took a charitable view of the opponents.

O Red Rose, O White Rose,
Set you but side by side,
And bring against you the leagued South,
You might their shock abide;
Yea, bring against you the branded South,
With all their strength allied.

My White Rose, my Red Rose

Could smite their puissance in the mouth!

This is echoed in a story told by the great Lancastrian cricket writer, Neville Cardus. Cardus was watching a Roses match at Headingley when a posh voice a few rows ahead called out: 'Why doesn't the bowlah bowl straight?'

A few minutes later: 'Why doesn't the battah hit the ball?'

Then, 'Why doesn't the skippah bring on a spinnah?'

Another voice rang out: 'Excuse me. Are tha' from Yorkshire?'

'No.'

'Are tha' from Lancashire?'

'No.'

'Well, what's it got to do wi' thee?'

Chapter 3

SCHOOL DAYS

FRANCIS THOMPSON'S parents were desperate for him to join the Roman Catholic priesthood and in 1870, just before his 11th birthday, he was sent to St Cuthbert's College, a seminary and boarding school at Ushaw, four miles from Durham. Francis remained an intelligent but solitary child. One of his teachers recalled a delicate-looking boy with a somewhat pinched expression of face, very quiet and unobtrusive, and perhaps a little melancholy. He was bullied by some of his classmates. 'The malignity of my tormentors was more heart-lacerating than the pain itself.'

A school friend recalled he was a good racquets player, but rarely played cricket, and if the ball came his way, he was usually somewhere else. He did recoup some credit with his schoolmates by reciting his poems, especially the humorous ones, in a loud voice.

His learning capacity was remarkable. By the age of 14 he could read, speak and write in Sanskrit and French and was fluent in Latin and Greek. He won 16 out of 21 school essay competitions. He did make some college friends, and a few tried to keep in touch when he later went to London, but he kept himself hidden.

Francis had gone to Ushaw determined to join the priesthood, but in his years there his literary ambitions took over. Eventually the school authorities decided he was not cut out for ordination, and the school president wrote to his parents advising them that he was not suited for the priesthood, citing his 'strong, nervous timidity' and a 'natural indolence'. He left Ushaw for home in July 1887.

His parents decided that if he was not to be a priest, he should follow his father into medicine. After a few months at home he passed examinations, some of them in Greek, to go to Owens College in Manchester to study to become a doctor. This did not work either. He wrote later that he hated his scientific and medical studies. He told a friend he could never stand the sight of flowing blood, though more recent biographers have offered a very different take on his attitude to bloodshed.

Instead, he spent much of his time walking the streets and visiting galleries and libraries, and he became a regular at Old Trafford. 'For several years, living within distance of the OT ground, where successively played each year the chief cricketers of England, where the chief cricketers of Australia played in their periodic visits, and where one of the three Australia Test matches was latterly decided, I saw all the great cricketers of the day, and it was a very rich day.' His early poems include recollections of heroes from Lancashire cricket, though the writing is a little overworked compared with his later masterpiece, *At Lord's*.

Sons who have sucked stern nature forth
From the milk of our firm-breasted north!
Stubborn and stark, in whatever field,
Stand, Sons of the Red Rose, who

    may not yield ...

Yet, though, Sugg, Eccles, Ward, Tyldesley play
The part of a great, a vanished day,
By this may ye know, and long may ye know,
Our Rose; it is greatest when hope is low.

In 1879 Francis suffered a long bout of fever and it was probably around then that his opium addiction began. He was treated with laudanum, a tincture of opium in alcohol used to treat a variety of conditions, including coughs. Until the early 20th century it was sold without prescription and was used in a range of painkillers. It was common among Manchester's cotton workers. Once it was proved to be addictive, it was strictly regulated.

It was also around this time that Francis's mother gave him a copy of Thomas de Quincey's *Confessions of an English Opium Eater*, published as a book in 1822. De Quincey died in Manchester in the year Francis was born. It's not clear why Francis's mother gave him the book, but he was already familiar with its contents, and she may have known about his enthusiasm for it. It was to be one of her last gifts. She died soon after, in December 1880.

The book explores both the horrors of the drug and what De Quincey describes as its creative power. Francis was particularly excited by the dream narratives which he called the book's crowning glory, and he regarded De Quincey with 'the feeling of a younger for an elder brother'.

After four years of study at Owens College he went to London and Glasgow for a series of examinations. Each time he told his family he had not passed the exams, but it's not clear if he had taken them. His father contacted the college authorities and was told his son was skipping more classes than he attended.

In 1883 Dr Thompson decided enough was enough and found other avenues for his son. He worked for a short time for a surgical instrument maker, then became an encyclopaedia salesman, but spent most of his time reading them, not selling them. He even enlisted in the army but failed to pass the physical test because his chest was too narrow. Life was more difficult for Francis because of his father's impending marriage to Annie Richardson, the daughter of a local clergyman, who did not get on with him. On Sunday, 8 November 1885 Francis, now aged 26, was confronted by his father about his drinking, stealing laudanum, or both. Francis vigorously defended himself. The following morning, he left one of his sisters a note saying he had gone to London.

Harry Newbolt and Clifton College were both 14 years old when he joined the school. His mother had moved the family into a large house within sight of the Close, and a gate at the corner gave him easy access from home. He belonged to North Town, one of the two houses for day boys. His education was largely in the classics, with some German and mathematics on the side. English literature was not on the curriculum, but Harry pursued it in his own time and claimed to have read Shakespeare and Sir Walter Scott through and through before he reached 14. He was also deeply immersed in Latin and at one point was summoned to see the headmaster to explain how he had done so well in a Latin exam without cheating. He explained that he knew Virgil's *Aeneid* off by heart.

His two most famous contemporaries at Clifton were Douglas, the future Field Marshal Earl Haig, and the writer Arthur Quiller-Couch. He was not close to either at school, though he and Quiller-Couch were poetic rivals. He got to know Haig later. Brother Frank was the star cricketer of the family. He was 6ft 3in tall by the time he reached 17 and made it into the school's first XI, unlike Harry, who admitted later that he had been an unreliable and second-rate player. His only moment of cricketing fame came with a winning performance as his house team skipper.

He did succeed in two solitary sports. He was skilled at shooting and was captain of the cadet corps and the shooting VIII. And he was a fine runner, specialising in sprinting and hurdling, though neither of these counted for much at cricket-obsessed Clifton. In December 1880 Harry and three schoolfriends went to Balliol College Oxford to try for a scholarship. The three friends won scholarships or exhibitions, with the income included. Harry was offered a place. He claimed later he had been close to scholarship success until he quoted from Tennyson's *In Memoriam*, which was viewed by the examiners as 'unorthodox'. In the end he tried for and won a scholarship at Corpus Christi, starting there in 1881.

Chapter 4

CLIFTON

There's a breathless hush in the Close to-night—
Ten to make and the match to win—
A bumping pitch and a blinding light,
An hour to play and the last man in.
And it's not for the sake of a ribboned coat,
Or the selfish hope of a season's fame,
But his captain's hand on his shoulder smote
'Play up! play up! and play the game!'

IN *THE TWYMANS*, Henry Newbolt's semi-
autobiographical novel of 1911, the hero Percy
arrives at Clifton (Downton in the book) for

the entrance examinations. 'In front lay a wide greensward, flooded with low sunlight, and covered in every direction with a multitude of white figures. Something broke over his spirit like a wave, a glimpse behind the mere beauty of the white young figures, of the long-descended discipline they symbolised.'

Founded in 1860 and formally opened in 1862, Clifton was one of a series of new schools to meet the needs of a burgeoning middle class. From the start, cricket was at its heart, with a school XI founded in its first summer in 1863.

The driving force behind Clifton's zeal for cricket was its second headmaster, John Percival, with the support of an assistant master. Newbolt was to write later that there were few members of the school who would not have bartered away all chance of intellectual distinction for a place in the cricket XI or the rugby XV.

He went on to rhapsodise in his autobiography, 'The days of our youth are the days of our glory – the hour, for example, of the glorious return of the Eleven from a Cheltenham match, when the road was dense with an expectant crowd who hurled themselves like a storming party upon the brake when it reached the top of College Road, took out the horses and brought the Eleven down the hill, hauling, cheering and swaying as if they were dragging a successful lifeboat ashore after a whole day's battling in danger of death.'

Apart from this, cricket barely gets a mention in his lengthy memoir, though he does compare the aggression of the Australian fast bowler, Fred 'The Demon' Spofforth, with the argumentative Greek philosopher Socrates. Spofforth had played on the Close in 1877 when Dave Gregory's Australian XI beat W.G. Grace's Gloucestershire.

Clifton's Junior School, for boys between 11 and 14, had two boarding houses, Clark's and Hartnell's, and two for day boys, North Town and South Town. From its foundation, day boys at Clifton enjoyed equal status with boarders, unlike their counterparts in the older public schools. A step out of the junior school led straight on to the Close.

In its early days the Clifton XI played local clubs and built up a regular fixture list with other schools, starting with Sherborne in 1865 and Cheltenham in 1872. From 1914 to 1968, Clifton was one of the original eight Lord's schools, who were entitled to play at cricket's headquarters. Their opponents were Tonbridge. The others were Cheltenham v. Haileybury, Rugby v. Marlborough and Eton v. Harrow.

In the early days Clifton's cricket profile was enhanced by its links with the great Bristolian, W.G. Grace. W.G. was past his schooldays when

Clifton opened but he sent two of his sons there, W.G. Jnr (Bertie), who captained the XI, and Charles Butler (Charlie). E.W. Swanton reckoned Clifton was Grace's favourite ground. His county, Gloucestershire, played at the Close for 50 years until the present county ground was built and W.G. scored 13 of his 126 centuries there, as many as he got in the rest of Gloucestershire put together and more than he scored anywhere except for Lord's and the Oval.

A number of Clifton cricketers made it all the way to the England Test team. One of them, Edward Tylecote, had already made his name in 1868 at the age of 19, playing in a school match. Batting for the Classics against the Moderns, he made 404 not out over three afternoons and six hours. After leaving Clifton, he was part of the Honourable Ivo Bligh's team sent to Australia in 1882/83 to recover the Ashes lost a few months earlier. England won the series 2-1 although there was some dispute about a fourth game, not part of the Ashes series, which the Australians won. A group of Melbourne ladies presented Bligh with an urn containing ashes with a poem attached:

When Ivo goes back with the urn, the urn.
Studds, Steel, Read and Tylecote return, return.
The welkin will ring loud,
The great crowd will feel proud,
Seeing Barlow and Bates with the urn, the urn
And the rest coming home with the urn

Another Cliftonian, Charles Lucas Townsend, was W.G. Grace's godson, and played for Gloucestershire under W.G. He was a leg-spinner who turned the ball viciously on the difficult wickets of the day. As he became more expensive, his batting blossomed and it was as an all-rounder that he played a couple of Tests against Australia in 1899. He was not a great success at Test level, but he did tour the United States under the captaincy of K.S. Ranjitsinhji.

James Kirtley, born in 1975, played in 11 one-day internationals, beginning in 2001. He made his Test debut in August 2003 against South Africa, and helped England to a 70-run victory, taking 6-34 in the second innings, including Graeme Smith, Jacques Rudolph and Mark Boucher. He played in three more Tests that year, against South Africa and on tour in Sri Lanka.

However, the most celebrated Clifton cricketer was not a future Test player but a 13-year-old schoolboy, A.E.J. (Arthur Edward Jeune) Collins. A.E.J. was born in India on 18 August 1885, the son of a judge in the Indian civil service. He was orphaned in India and was adopted by family guardians in Tavistock, Devon, who sent him to board at Clifton. His arrival at the school in 1897 coincided with the publication of Newbolt's slim collection, *Admirals All*, including *Vitai Lampada* with its Close nostalgia.

On Thursday, 22 June 1899, young A.E.J., skipper of the Clark's House XI, led his team across Guthrie Road and on to the Junior School pitch to face the North Town Junior XI. Collins's team was made up of six 13-year-olds, four 14-year-olds and one 12-year-old. The North Team was younger, with one 14-year-old, four aged 13, four aged 12 and one aged 11.

Collins won the toss and chose to bat. The pitch was irregular and comparatively small. The boundary on one side was relatively short, so a boundary was worth only two runs. The other side had no boundary line at all so everything had to be run. In the two and a half hours of play on that first Thursday, Collins, opening with A.M. Champion, had reached exactly 200 runs when the bell for pre-supper prep rang at 6.30. In another two and a half hours on Friday,

Collins took his own score to 509, thanks in part to a dropped catch by the nervous 11-year-old, Victor Fuller Eberle. After a weekend off, play resumed on Monday, but lessons allowed only 55 minutes of play.

By now news of Collins's feat was spreading across parliament, the press and the empire. Collins and number 11 Tom Redfern resumed on Tuesday. Collins was starting to flag and was dropped a couple of times, but the innings finally ended with Redfern caught by young Eberle. Collins had reached 628 not out in just under seven hours, comprising 146 boundaries (two runs each), a six, four fives, 30 fours and 36 threes, all of them run. The 'Limp Pocket Scorebook', still on display in the Preparatory School Library, reports that in reply North Town could make only 148 in their two innings, Collins taking 11 wickets for 63 runs. The precision of the original scorebook can't be tested and

Collins's score could be plus or minus 20. Either way, it was a record.

Suggestions that the North Town team collaborated in prolonging Collins's innings were strongly denied by Eberle, later captain of the college's first XI, who insisted that the match was played 'in the traditional spirit of house rivalry and keenness'. Eberle complained that he had been unpopular both for dropping Collins, then for catching Redfern and bringing the drama to a close.

In the years that followed, Collins excelled in all sports, representing the school in rackets and rugby as well as cricket. He scored 112 in his last match for the Clifton first XI against the Old Cliftonians. He continued to play after entering the Royal Military Academy at Woolwich until he was gazetted as a lieutenant and posted to India with the 2nd Sappers and Miners in 1907. He did manage to play for the Old Cliftonians when on a home posting to Britain and made another century. By 1913 his regiment was back in England and the following spring he married Ethel Slater, the daughter of a retired army officer, in a ceremony near Castletown on the Isle of Man.

They were not together for long. In August the Great War broke out and Collins was among the first to leave with the British Expeditionary Force to France. He was mortally wounded during the first battle of Ypres on 11 November and was taken back to the trenches but did not survive. He was buried in an unmarked grave, but his name is recorded on the Menin Gate. He was not the only member of his family to die in the conflict. Two brothers also perished. Of the 22 boys who played in the famous house match of 1899, 16 went to war and did not return.

Collins's record remained unbroken for over a century until it was surpassed in 2016 by a 15-year-old Indian schoolboy. Pranav Dhanawade, the son of an auto rickshaw driver, scored 1,009 runs over two days, 14–15 January, playing for KC Gandhi High School against Arya Gurukul School in Mumbai. The match was part of the Bhandari Cup, an under-16 competition recognised by the Mumbai Cricket Association.

Arya Gurukul batted first and they were skittled for 31 in 20 overs. KC Gandhi replied with 1,465/3, declaring at 3pm on day two. Pranav Dhanawade's contribution included 59 sixes and 129 fours. Batting again, Arya Gurukul were bowled out for 52.

Their coach admitted they had had a difficult time getting a team together because of exams and had turned up to avoid being dropped from the tournament in future. He calculated that his fielders had dropped 21 catches and missed three stumpings, and revealed that some of his boys, many of them under 12, had only played cricket with a tennis ball and were scared of the harder leather ball.

But Dhanawade's extraordinary innings was an indisputable record for an officially recognised match. Congratulations flooded in from superstars like Sachin Tendulkar and Mahendra Singh Dhoni, and the minister of sport for Maharashtra rewarded Dhanawade by promising to pay for his future education and coaching.

Chapter 5

NEW RISEN LANCASHIRE

It is little I repair to the matches of the
    Southron folk,
Though my own red roses there may blow;
It is little I repair to the matches of the
    Southron folk,
Though the red roses crest the caps, I know.
For the field is full of shades as I near a
    shadowy coast,
And a ghostly batsman plays to the
    bowling of a ghost,
And I look through my tears on a soundless-
    clapping host

As the run stealers flicker to and fro,

To and fro:

O my Hornby and my Barlow long ago!

THE GAME in Lancashire gradually took off in the opening years of the 19th century but the early days are misty. There had been a match on 1 September 1781, played on Brinnington Moor in Cheshire and reported in the press, involving a team made up of men from Haughton in Lancashire and Bredbury in Cheshire. Their opponents were gentlemen from the printing business.

Local legend has it that a match was played on a field off Cazneau Street in Liverpool towards the end of the 18th century. Folklore on the Lancashire coast claims that the Fylde Cricket Club was founded in 1810, but there is no documented proof of either of these stories. The first club known to have been founded was the Original and Unrivalled Mosslake Fields Cricket Society, born in Liverpool in 1807. The team played on five grounds across the city before moving to Aigburth, which is still Liverpool CC's cricket headquarters. Liverpool was effectively the birthplace of Lancashire cricket, but over the next few decades more clubs were founded in Manchester, Broughton, Rochdale, Burnley, Preston, Ribblesdale, Blackburn, Lancaster and other towns and villages.

Lancashire was a heavily industrialised county, and this was a serious drag on the spread of the game. The long working hours in the cotton mills, including a full day on Saturdays, left most of the population with no time for cricket. This was very much the view of the sports outfitter and cricket entrepreneur, Frederick Lillywhite, 'Lancashire boasts many good cricketers but from the fact that most of its towns being manufacturing, the residents have little or no time to devote to this noble pastime.'

Life became easier in 1847 with the passing at Westminster of the Ten Hours Act, which limited the working week to 55 and a half hours, leaving Saturday afternoon free and giving a lift to organised sports. Brian Bearshaw's *From the Stretford End* quotes from the diary of Rossendale cotton-spinner Moses Heap. 'For a while we did not know how to pass our time away. Before, it had been all bed and work. Now, in place of seventy hours a week, we had fifty-five and a half hours. It became a practice, mostly on Saturdays, to play games, especially football and cricket, which had never been done before.'

The spread of the game across the county was not universally welcomed. In 1832 the Primitive Methodist Church in Haslingden echoed the view of the 17th-century Puritans, 'If any teacher be found guilty of Sabbath-breaking, frequenting public houses, card tables, dancing rooms, cricket-playing or gaming of any kind, or any other practice contrary to the Word of God, they shall be admonished for their conduct. If they repent, well; if not, they shall be expelled from the Society.'

The early years also saw some curious novelty games. In 1838 the Manchester Cricket Club ground at Hulme hosted a match between two teams from the club. The first XI comprised 11 players. The second XI was made up of ten players and a bowling machine called a 'catapulter'. The catapulter took two early wickets but then broke down and had to retire, ceding victory to the first XI. In 1863 another Manchester ground saw a match between 11 one-legged men and 11 one-armed men. The *Manchester Courier* reported that both sides played with skill and agility.

By the 1850s, the three leading clubs in Lancashire were Manchester, Liverpool and Broughton. In 1856 Manchester had to leave its ground to make way for the Manchester art treasures exhibition. The club agreed to vacate its home on condition that the owner, Sir Humphrey de Trafford, provided it with a new location. In the end it was given a new ground a quarter of a mile away, the site of today's Old Trafford. The art exhibition was opened by Prince Albert on 5 May 1857. The prince returned to the show on 30 June with Queen Victoria and a cohort of royals including Prince Frederick William of Prussia. Over the 142 days the exhibition was open, more than a million people paid to view it. Interest in Manchester cricket was minimal by comparison.

If Lancashire club cricket had been slow to develop, the county game was no quicker. By 1864, the year of the legalisation of over-arm bowling and the first edition of *Wisden*, there were eight major county teams: Kent, Sussex, Surrey, Hampshire, Middlesex, Yorkshire, Nottinghamshire and Cambridgeshire. The drive to launch a Lancashire county team was headed by members of the Manchester club. Three of them called a meeting on 12 January at the Queen's Hotel in Manchester. Thirteen clubs were represented: four from Manchester, three from Liverpool, and the others from Ashton, Blackburn, Accrington, Wigan, Whalley and Oldham. There were no representatives from the north of the county.

The plan adopted by the meeting was to hold matches in Manchester, Liverpool, Preston, Blackburn and other grounds, but this did not last long, as Manchester gradually grew to dominate the county club. This in turn alienated clubs across Lancashire, who rated their own fixtures as superior.

In its first year, Lancashire played against a number of local clubs and its first county games came in 1865, with home and away fixtures against Middlesex. The following year Surrey agreed to meet them and in 1867 the first

Roses match against Yorkshire was played at Whalley.

Two major problems beset the county. Compared with other county sides, Lancashire relied heavily on amateurs, so the reluctance of gentlemen players to travel made selection for away matches difficult. The treatment of professionals also caused some anger. A *Manchester Courier* reader asked, 'How do men like to be thrust out of the society of gentlemen with whom they have been playing the levelling game, par excellence, immediately the dinner bell rings, into a frowsy hole to eat their bit of bread and cheese as best they can?' A writer in the *Manchester and Salford Gazette*, William E. Hodkinson, took a similar line, 'I cannot for the life of me understand why the gentlemen should be worshipped so much as to have the entire possession of the pavilion while the players (who are equally as much to be depended upon for winning a match) should be thrown away as "dirt" into an old "cow shed" on the right-hand side of the field to don their flannels etc.'

There was also continued resentment among local clubs at what they saw as a takeover of the county side by the Manchester club. Club cricket in the county continued to thrive. Through the 1870s huge crowds turned up at Broughton to see festival matches against W.G. Grace and the United South. Attendance at the Lancashire versus Surrey match at Old Trafford on the same days was paltry. The numbers at Broughton were boosted by a large contingent of lady promenaders. At Old Trafford the number of women spectators was usually under a dozen.

By the early 1870s the game at club level had grown rapidly. The *City News* wrote of the occupation of nearly every vacant piece of ground by boys engaged in cricket of an evening, with a few bricks for a wicket. But the county struggled and in 1871 only two counties, Hampshire and Sussex, would play them. Gloucestershire and W.G. Grace turned them down year after year. But by the end of the decade the county game was becoming more popular in Lancashire and the prestige of the side was growing. In 1878 the touring Australians played at Old Trafford. Later that season came the great leap forward. W.G. relented and Gloucestershire came north.

Chapter 6

MEAN STREETS

FRANCIS THOMPSON'S first three years
in London were a time of destitution and rough
sleeping.

His father sent him a weekly allowance, but
he stopped collecting it. He gave up a job working
for a bookseller and instead picked up handouts
in the street for selling matches, blacking boots
and holding the reins of carriage horses. He slept
in wooden boxes in shelters or in the open air,
and frequented the Guildhall Library until the
management decided he was too scruffy, and
he was barred. The young assistant responsible,

Bernard Kettle, admitted later that he'd been entertaining an angel unawares.

In December 1886, Thompson, off the drugs and smartly dressed, went back to Ashton-under-Lyne to spend Christmas with the family. But he soon headed back to London and the drugs. He was to write about this period a decade later: 'These horrible streets, with their gangrenous multitudes, blackening ever into lower mortifications of humanity! The brute men; these lads who have almost lost the faculty of human speech, who howl and growl like animals, or use a tongue which is itself a cancerous disintegration of speech.' He also wrote of 'girls whose practice is a putrid ulceration of love'. It was one of these 'girls' who rescued him for a while, sharing her home and her income with him. He called her his saviour. 'O brave, sad, sad, lovingest, tender thing,' he wrote.

He also had help from a boot-shop owner, John McMaster, a devout Anglican who looked after the derelict and homeless, but Thompson's laudanum habit caused problems and he was asked to leave after injuring a customer by slamming a window shutter on his foot.

A more lasting change began in February 1887, when he sent some of his poetry and prose to Wilfred Meynell, the editor of a monthly Catholic literary magazine, *Merry England*. It took Meynell six months to get round to reading it. During that period, Thompson attempted suicide with an overdose of opium but was deterred, he said, by the ghost of the young poet, Thomas Chatterton, who had killed himself a century before.

Once Meynell had finally read the work, he tried to reach Thompson but without success, so he published one of his poems in *Merry England*. Thompson heard about it and wrote back. Meynell finally made contact through Thompson's poste restante, a chemist's shop in

Drury Lane, and invited him to his house for a meeting. He turned up in rags, with no shirt and his stockingless feet showing through his boots. Meynell found him a home, food and medical care, and was to be his protector for the rest of his life.

Thompson's other guardian was Meynell's wife Alice, a journalist and poet who was rumoured to be on the list for Poet Laureate when Alfred Tennyson died in 1892. She became Thompson's guide and inspiration. His feelings for her were a mixture of love and worship, emotions which were inseparable for Thompson.

His first meeting with Meynell brought his relationship with the prostitute to an end. Meynell's son Everard, Thompson's early biographer, says he went home to the girl and told her about his new friends. He wondered whether he should stay with her but she told him, 'They will not understand our friendship.' Without warning, she disappeared into new lodgings. He walked the streets looking for her but never saw her again.

The rest of Thompson's life became a cycle of laudanum, the pains of withdrawal, the flow of poetry and back to the laudanum. The Meynells found him a refuge for a while at a priory at Storrington, West Sussex, but the isolation was too much for him and rooms were found for him in Queen's Park, west London. By 1892 he was back on the drug, and his guardians sent him off to a Franciscan monastery at Pantasaph in Flintshire for more rehabilitation. Once again, his writing flowed and in December 1893 his first volume of poetry, entitled simply *Poems* was published, to critical acclaim.

It included his most famous religious work, *The Hound of Heaven*, which he had begun at Storrington, and which had appeared in *Merry England*. It recounts, in a complex and florid

style, God's pursuit of a man fleeing from Him
in ignorance:

I fled Him down the nights and down the days;

I fled Him down the arches of the years;

I fled Him, down the labyrinthine ways

Of my own mind, and in the mist of tears

I hid from Him, and under running laughter.

Up vistaed hopes I sped,

And shot, precipitated,

Adown Titanic glooms of chasmed fears

From those strong Feet that followed,

   followed after

But with unhurrying chase,

And unperturbed pace,

Deliberate speed, majestic instancy,

They beat – and a Voice beat

More instant than the Feet –

All things betray thee, who betrayest Me.

Chapter 7

MARGARET

AS A STUDENT at Oxford Henry Newbolt
indulged in a little self-parody, reciting Cicero
while floating on a punt down the Cherwell. But
he did get a first in his second-year exams, along
with his friend Anthony Hawkins, later known as
Anthony Hope, author of *The Prisoner of Zenda*.
To embellish his literary image, he moved into
rooms vacated by the elderly writer and scholar
John Ruskin.

He played a range of sports, rowing, running
and some impromptu football, but no cricket.
And he went to dances with the young ladies of

Oxford, many of them the daughters of dons. In the summer of his third year he fell in love with Beatrice Mueller, the daughter of the Leipzig-born academic Max Mueller, who was Oxford's first Professor of Comparative Philology.

He began his fourth year confident he would get a first. But he damaged his chances by pulling out of a viva – a live exam – to take part in a sprint race, and ended up with a second, to his own and his family's distress. His failure to get a first meant a junior academic post was out of the question. He might have been offered a teaching job at Clifton, but he decided 'I will not be a pedagogue.' The Church and the army did not appeal, and business was out of the question for someone of his class.

He turned to the law and was offered a place as a pupil with chambers at Lincoln's Inn. He made steady progress and was soon earning money in court. He also went in for court reporting and reckoned he was making more as a journalist than as a lawyer. While all this was going on, he was enjoying a hectic social life. There were parties and balls including one at which he met William Gladstone, Lord Acton and Oscar Wilde on the same night.

And there were long visits to stay with friends around the country. It was on one of these outings that his life changed. He and his sister Milly boarded a train at Dorking in Surrey and joined a party on their way to Lynton in Devon. When they reached Yeovil in Somerset a young woman called Margaret Duckworth joined the train. Within hours Newbolt was in love.

Margaret was a very attractive woman who rode fast horses and outpaced the men striding over the moors. She was as deeply into science and philosophy as she was into what were then regarded as feminine subjects such as music. Newbolt decided he wanted to marry her, and a mutual friend said she would take a letter from him to Margaret's father.

The Reverend Arthur Duckworth owned Orchardleigh, a large estate near Frome in Somerset. In her 1997 biography of Newbolt, Susan Chitty relates how father and suitor met and Arthur Duckworth decided Newbolt was a suitable match. But Margaret said no. The reason was her relationship with someone else, her cousin Ella Coltman. Ella was a beautiful woman, a year older than Margaret. She belonged to a club called The Grecians, a group of young women determined to break into the male stronghold of the classics.

Newbolt had to bide his time. Finally, Chitty relates, he met Ella by chance at a party. He was charmed by her. He also knew that Margaret would only accept him if Ella was included in the relationship. Fortunately, Ella was suitably impressed by Newbolt. The following August,

Margaret joined the train at Yeovil again. Next morning, she and Henry walked together to the sea and came back to announce their engagement. The next step was for Newbolt to visit Margaret's family at Orchardleigh. Life at the house was rather grand with partridge shooting and a choice of four ports at dinner. Margaret also visited Newbolt's family. She and Emily were not close, but Margaret thought she, Henry, Frank and Milly were a happy quartet.

Frank married in November 1888 and Milly a month later. Meanwhile, Margaret and Henry went house-hunting and found a home in South Kensington, a cheaper area than Mayfair, but becoming more popular now that the Metropolitan underground line reached Gloucester Road. They were married on 15 August 1889 in the Island Chapel at Orchardleigh and spent the first night of their honeymoon in Dorset. Margaret was to write later, 'There still comes back to me the naturalness of our wedding night.'

There remained a third party in the marriage and Newbolt kept his promise to include Ella in the relationship. He wrote to her describing waking up with Margaret, an experience familiar to Ella. After Henry and Margaret moved into their new home Ella at once became part of the family. Margaret spent weekdays at the Coltman family home and Ella spent most of her evenings with the Newbolts before taking a hansom cab home.

Eventually Ella complained to Henry that she was feeling excluded. They solved the problem by becoming lovers. Margaret knew about the relationship but neither she nor Ella appeared to resent the other. The Newbolts' first child, Celia, was born nine months after the wedding. On 3 March 1893 Margaret gave birth to her second child, a son, Francis. The trio agreed that he should be known as Ella's child.

The Grecian Club continued its studies. Margaret and Celia were joined by Mary Coleridge, great-great-niece of Samuel Taylor. Henry took Thursday afternoons off to join in the reading and writing.

In 1892 he published his first novel, *Taken from the Enemy*, a thriller in the style of Robert Louis Stevenson, about a plot to rescue Napoleon from St Helena.

Newbolt was also continuing his legal work, giving advice to, among others, a young man called Guglielmo Marconi, a cousin of Mary's, and inventor of the wireless. Guglielmo had travelled from Bologna and was negotiating a rather naive deal with a firm offering to invest in his new invention, the oscillating aerial. Newbolt put him in touch with William Henry Preece, an inventor from Caernarvon and chief electrical engineer of the British Post Office. Marconi never looked back.

During the domestic drama, Newbolt's literary career took off. In 1895, *Longman's Magazine* published his ballad of the sea, *Admirals All*. The verses tell the tales of eight British naval heroes:

Effingham, Grenville, Raleigh, Drake,
Here's to the bold and free!
Benbow, Collingwood, Byron, Blake,
Hail to the Kings of the Sea!

The poem is pure Newbolt, blending patriotism, militarism and a dim view of foreigners:

Drake nor devil nor Spaniard feared,
Their cities he put to the sack,
He singed his Catholic Majesty's beard
And harried his ships to wrack.

Newbolt concluded:

But they left us a kingdom none can take –

The realm of the circling sea –

To be ruled by the rightful sons of Blake,

And the Rodneys yet to be.

Admirals All was a critical and popular success, but it was upstaged in January 1897 by the publication in an evening paper, the *St James's Gazette*, of another ballad, *Drake's Drum*.

Drake he's in his hammock an' a

    thousand mile away

Capten, art tha sleepin' there below?

Slung atween the round shot in

    Nombre Dios Bay,

An' dreamin' arl the time o' Plymouth Hoe.

These sea songs were given a lift by Kaiser Wilhelm II, who had been building up the German naval fleet, pushing Britain into sending out a special service squadron. Drake's Drum was a sensation. Newbolt told how he had walked home from work passing dozens of newspaper vendors crying out the ballad's name. It was to become a big hit when set to music by Charles Villiers Stanford.

Call him on the deep sea, call him up the Sound,
Call him when ye sail to meet the foe,
Where the old trade's plyin' an' the old flag flyin',
They shall find him, ware an' wakin' as they
     found him long ago.

Newbolt was winning more literary friends, including the ageing Poet Laureate, Robert Bridges, who introduced him to an up-and-coming Irish poet, W.B. Yeats. The three of them lunched at Bridges' house and Yeats was forced to play cricket.

Newbolt's poems finally appeared in book form in 1897. The collection was part of a series edited by the poet and scholar, Laurence Binyon, who was determined to turn the tide against what he regarded as the 'decadent' poetry of the period.

The book, including *Admirals All*, *Drake's Drum* and other ballads of the sea came out on Trafalgar Day, 2 October, to rapturous reviews in the *Daily Mail*, the *Daily Chronicle* and other newspapers and magazines. It sold more than 20,000 copies. Bridges urged Newbolt to quit the law. Newbolt hesitated but continued to churn out ballads at the rate of one a fortnight. He called himself a sausage machine. Gallantry at sea was a common theme, but not all the poems had a naval inspiration. Among the non-naval pieces in *Admirals All* was one of its most enduring, *Vitai Lampada*.

Chapter 8

WHILE THE
CHURCH APPROVES ...

'It is hard to tell where the MCC ends, and the
Church of England begins.'

J.B. Priestley

THE COUNTIES were free to decide on the
constitution of the Championship, but the rules,
or Laws of the Game, remained in the hands of
Marylebone Cricket Club. The Laws had been
under MCC's jurisdiction for nearly a century and
would remain there for as long again.

The origins of MCC remain in the mists. Many of its players are thought to have come from the White Conduit Club in Islington, north London. The new club appears to have been launched at the Star and Garter, a posh pub in Pall Mall, where a group of well-to-do players and supporters had drafted the Laws of Cricket in 1744 and again in 1774. The team played at several grounds including White Conduit Fields, but the Fields were open to the public, which left the players vulnerable to barracking from the lower orders. So the members asked a cricket-loving Yorkshire businessman named Thomas Lord to build them a ground. His first pitch was in Dorset Square to the north of Marylebone.

In 1787 it hosted a match between men of the Mary-le-Bone club and the Islington club. MCC was to declare this as its official founding date.

The lease on the ground ran out in 1810 and Lord opened a new venue nearby on the St John's estate. This only lasted a few years before parliament approved a route for the new Regent's Canal to flow right through it. MCC finally found a permanent home nearby in St John's Wood, and played their first match there on 22 June 1814, beating Hertfordshire by an innings and 21 runs.

When the International Cricket Council (ICC) was formed in 1909 (then called the Impreial Cricket Conference), MCC secretary Francis Lacey became ICC chairman, an arrangement which survived till 1989. For most of the 20th century, from the Australia tour of 1903/04 to the India tour of 1976/77, the England team was called MCC except for Test matches.

Membership of MCC was precious and could take 25 years to achieve, unless one was prime minister or a superstar like Sir Mick

Jagger. E.W. Swanton, not usually thought of as a radical, reckoned there was no democracy involved and membership of the aristocracy was more important than cricketing ability.

Women were banned from membership until the 1990s when former England captain Rachael Heyhoe Flint applied to join as R. Flint. Change finally came when Colin Ingleby-Mackenzie was made president in 1996 and pushed for female membership.

Some members stuck to the view that MCC was a gentlemen's club and should remain that way. Besides, it was argued, the facilities for gentlemen members were already stretched. In particular, it was felt gentlemen should not have to share toilets with women. On the other side, the journalist and broadcaster Michael Parkinson suggested that the entire pavilion be converted into a public toilet to accommodate male and female members without embarrassment. It would also stop play being held up by movement behind the bowler's arm. In September 1998 a 70 per cent majority voted for change, just over the two-thirds needed to end 212 years of male exclusivity.

The atmosphere at Lord's a century ago was captured by the war hero, war-hater and cricket fanatic, Siegfried Sassoon, under the name Solly Sizzum. The title of the poem may be ambiguous:

THE BLUES AT LORD'S
Near-neighboured by a blandly boisterous Dean
Who 'hasn't missed the Match since 92,'
Proposing to perpetuate the scene
I concentrate my eyesight on the cricket.
The game proceeds, as it is bound to do
Till tea-time or the fall of the next wicket.

Agreeable sunshine fosters greensward greener
Than College lawns in June. Tradition-true,

The stalwart teams, capped with contrasted blue,

Exert their skill; adorning the arena

With modest, manly, muscular demeanour, —

Reviving memories in ex-athletes who

Are superannuated from agility, —

And (while the five-ounce fetish they pursue)

Admired by gloved and virginal gentility.

My intellectual feet approach this function

With tolerance and Public-School compunction;

Aware that, whichsoever side bats best,

Their partisans are equally well-dressed.

For, though the Government has gone vermilion

And, as a whole, is weak in Greek and Latin,

The fogies harboured by the august Pavilion

Sit strangely similar to those who sat in

That edifice when first the Dean went pious, —

For possible preferment sacrificed

His hedonistic and patrician bias,

And offered his complacency to Christ.

Meanwhile some Cantab slogs a fast half-volley

Against the ropes. 'Good shot, sir! O good shot!'

Ejaculates the Dean in accents jolly…

Will Oxford win? Perhaps. Perhaps they'll not.

Can Cambridge lose? Who knows? One

    fact seems sure;

That, while the Church approves,

    Lord's will endure.

Chapter 9

GRACE BROTHERS

It's Glo'ster coming North, the irresistible,

The Shire of the Graces long ago!

It's Gloucestershire up North, the irresistible,

And new-risen Lancashire the foe!

A shire so young that has scarce

impressed its traces,

Ah, how shall it stand before all-

resistless Graces?

O, little red rose, their bats are as maces

To beat thee down, this summer long ago!

FRANCIS THOMPSON'S *All Resistless Graces*
were E.M. and W.G., always known by their
initials, and G.F., known to everyone as Fred.
They were sons of Dr Henry Mills Grace, the
father of a cricketing family and a cricketing
county.

Gloucestershire had known forerunners of
cricket like stool-ball, or stob-ball, in the 16th
century, but the first recorded game in the county
was played in Gloucester in 1729. Very little
cricket is recorded after that until well into the
next century.

Henry Grace was born in 1808 at Long
Ashton in Somerset. He studied medicine and
practised in Bristol, where he married Martha
Pocock in 1831. They had 11 children, six sons
and five daughters, the start of a remarkable
cricketing dynasty. In all, 13 sons and grandsons
played cricket. Add the nephews and cousins –
two Gilberts, two Pococks and three Reeses –

and there were nearly enough for a full match. Henry Mills died in 1871.

Henry founded Mangotsfield Cricket Club on the eastern outskirts of Bristol in the 1860s, and later joined up with Coalpit Heath to form West Gloucestershire. It renamed itself as the county club in 1867 but had a rival in the Cheltenham and Gloucester club. Thursday, 25 June 1868 saw Henry Grace's side play its first match as the county side, a two-dayer against MCC at Lord's. W.G., E.M. and Fred were all in the team which won by 134 runs.

The first official first-class match came two years later, against Surrey at Durdham Down, Clifton, a three-dayer beginning on Wednesday, 2 June. Again, the three brothers all turned out for Gloucestershire, and they won by 51 runs. The following year the club merged with the Cheltenham and Gloucester side and Gloucestershire County Cricket Club was finally up and running.

The oldest of the three Grace brothers was Edward Mills Grace, or Ted to his family and E.M. to everyone else. He was born in 1841 in Downend near Bristol and was one of the great cricketers of the 1860s and 1870s. His outstanding performance came in 1862 playing for MCC against Kent. He carried his bat through the first innings in making 192 out of a total of 344, then took 10-69 in Kent's first innings. It was a 12-a-side match so was not officially recognised. After the 1863 season E.M. toured America with George Parr's XI, then sailed to Australia and New Zealand with the All-England team.

He left the game while he studied medicine, later becoming a coroner, but returned in 1871 to the newly formed Gloucestershire county club. Led by him and his brothers, Gloucestershire were county champions in 1874, 1876 and 1877 and shared the title in 1873. The trio also played in the first Test match in England at the Oval in 1880, the only time three brothers have played for England in the same Test. E.M. was married four times and fathered 18 children. He died in 1911 at the age of 69.

G.F. or Fred was the youngest of the Grace family, born in 1850. Like E.M. and W.G. he learned the game in the old orchard at the family home under the tutelage of his father and his uncle, Alfred Pocock, and with the encouragement of the family's driving force, his mother Martha, E.M. had learned to play using a full-sized bat which was too big for him, and he developed a tendency to play across the line. The two younger brothers used smaller bats and played straight.

Fred turned out for his father's West Gloucestershire side in 1864 at the age of 13, and two years later he made his first-class debut playing for the Gentlemen of England against

Oxford University Cricket Club at the Magdalen ground. In the years that followed he played for his father's side as it progressed to the status of Gloucestershire county, and toured Australia with W.G.'s team in 1873/74.

In 1880 he was selected to play against the Australian touring side at the Oval in the first Test match in England. He was out for a duck in both innings, becoming the first batsman to be out for a pair in a Test. He made up for it by catching the massive Australian batsman George Bonnor. Bonnor hit the ball high in the air and the batsmen were into their third run when Fred took what was to be called 'the most famous deep field catch in history'.

Fred caught a cold during the match, and it worsened after he was soaked by rain twice while playing a family fixture at Stroud. A couple of days later he travelled to Basingstoke en route to a match at Winchester. He took a room at the

Red Lion Hotel, but his health deteriorated. His brother Henry and his cousin Walter Gilbert came to see him and Gilbert stayed on.

On Wednesday, 22 September his condition became even worse. W.G. and other family members set off to Basingstoke, but while they waited for a train at Bradford-on-Avon, word reached them that Fred had died. He was 29 years old. The cause of death was given as congestion of the lungs – pneumonia. At the funeral 3,000 people followed the coffin. The Australians wore black armbands on the first day of their final match that day.

When Arthur Conan Doyle was not writing about Sherlock Holmes or attending séances, he played cricket. His hero's name was borrowed from a cricketer.

'Years ago, I made thirty runs against a bowler by the name of Sherlock, and I always had a kindly feeling for that name,' he said. Conan Doyle played in 412 matches for more than 50 teams. His regular appearances were with Portsmouth (49), Hampshire Rovers (26), Norwood (71) and, top of the list, MCC, with 96. He played ten first-class matches, primarily as a batsman, and as a bowler he only took one first-class wicket.

In retrospect, there is a strange inevitability about the fact that it was the wicket of W.G. Grace. Conan Doyle was captaining MCC against Grace and the London County XI. He brought on seven bowlers against Grace but W.G. cruised past his hundred so Conan Doyle decided on an experimental over himself. It came off. He threw up a half volley outside the off stump with the fielders packed on the off, tempting Grace to sweep. For once he got a top edge and the ball went straight up and back down into the hands of the wicketkeeper, Storer of Derbyshire. Conan Doyle recalled, 'The old man laughed and shook his head at me. He was thinking that probably it was the worst ball that ever took his wicket, but he was too polite to say so. He turned over his right shoulder while he glared back and rambled all sorts of comminations.'

Conan Doyle reminisced about Grace in a memoir published in the *Strand* magazine in July 1927, 11 years after W.G.'s death on 23 October 1915. He imagines a young Grace, tall and slim with a black bushy beard and a high-pitched voice with a West Country burr. But he remembers an older Grace, tall but stooping, very stout, still with the black beard and the high voice. He writes that towards the end of his career he looked slow, stiff and heavy at the start of an innings. By the time he passed 50 he looked younger and fresher. As he reached a century, he was watching the ball with as clear an eye as in the first over. His command of the off-side ball and his perfect defence were his great strengths, but with his good eye he played more strokes to leg than any other batsman of his day. The only shot he played less than his contemporaries was the big hit for six, which he thought could end up on the pavilion roof or in the hands of cover.

As a bowler he was an innovator. Conan Doyle reckons he invented leg theory a century before it became common. He lumbered up to the wicket in a take-it-or-leave-it manner which covered up his great accuracy and command of length.

Conan Doyle spends little time on Grace's less appealing side – the shamateurism which brought him more money than any professional, or his truculence with umpires, though he does accept that he was more irritable as he got older. But he sees him as 'the very impersonation of cricket – redolent of fresh air, of good humour, of conflict without malice, of chivalrous strife, of keenness for victory by fair means and utter detestation of all that were foul'.

It's hard to imagine two more contrasting characters than W.G. Grace and Sherlock Holmes, and Conan Doyle turned to verse to recall his confrontation with the grouchy giant.

A REMINISCENCE OF CRICKET

Once in my heyday of cricket,

One day I shall ever recall!

I captured that glorious wicket,

The greatest, the grandest of all.

Before me he stands like a vision,

Bearded and burly and brown,

A smile of good humoured derision

As he waits for the first to come down.

A statue from Thebes or from Knossos,

A Hercules shrouded in white,

Assyrian bull-like colossus,

He stands in his might.

With the beard of a Goth or a Vandal,

His bat hanging ready and free,

His great hairy hands on the handle,

And his menacing eyes upon me.

And I – I had tricks for the rabbits,

The feeble of mind or eye,

I could see all the duffer's bad habits

And where his ruin might lie.

The capture of such might elate one,

But it seemed like one horrible jest

That I should serve tosh to the great one,

Who had broken the hearts of the best.

Well, here goes! Good Lord, what a rotter!

Such a sitter as never was dreamt;

It was clay in the hands of the potter,

But he tapped it with quiet contempt.

The second was better – a leetle;

It was low, but was nearly long-hop;

As the housemaid comes down on the beetle

So down came the bat with a chop.

He was sizing me up with some wonder,

My broken-kneed action and ways;

I could see the grim menace from under

The striped peak that shaded his gaze.

The third was a gift or it looked it –

A foot off the wicket or so;

His huge figure swooped as he hooked it,

His great body swung to the blow.

Still when my dreams are night-marish,

I picture that terrible smite,

It was meant for a neighbouring parish,

Or any place out of sight.

But – yes, there's a but to the story –

The blade swished a trifle too low;

Oh wonder, and vision of glory!

It was up like a shaft from a bow.

Up, up like a towering game bird,

Up, up to a speck in the blue,

And then coming down like the same bird,

Dead straight on the line that it flew.

Good Lord, it was mine! Such a soarer

Would call for a safe pair of hands;

None safer than Derbyshire Storer,

And there, face uplifted, he stands

Wicket keep Storer, the knowing,

Wary and steady of nerve,

Watching it falling and growing

Marking the pace and curve.

I stood with my two eyes fixed on it,

Paralysed, helpless, inert;

There was 'plunk' as the gloves shut upon it,

And he cuddled it up to his shirt.

Out – beyond question or wrangle!

Homeward he lurched to his lunch!

His bat was tucked up at an angle,

His great shoulders curved to a hunch.

Walking he rumbled and grumbled,

Scolding himself and not me;

One glove was off, and he fumbled,

Twisting the other hand free

Did I give Storer the credit

The thanks he so splendidly earned?

It was mere empty talk if I said it,

For Grace had already returned.

Chapter 10

MONKEY AND STONEWALL

ONE OF the more telling, if comical, images of class division in Victorian England is the picture of two opening batsmen stepping out on to the pitch to start an innings. One emerges from a grand pavilion at one end of the ground, the other from a wooden cabin at the opposite end. This was for many seasons a routine for Dick Barlow and A.N. Hornby who, thanks to Francis Thompson, are on the list of legendary opening pairs along with the likes of Hobbs and Sutcliffe, Greenidge and Haynes and Hutton and Washbrook.

For Hornby, cricket was a game. For Barlow it was a game and a job. Born in 1847, Hornby was the son of a business and political family. Barlow was born to a working-class family in Bolton in 1850.

Albert Neilson Hornby was the sixth son of William Henry Hornby, a cotton mill owner and MP for Blackburn from 1857 to 1865. W.H. was unseated after an allegation of bribery by his agent. Another son, E.K., won the election which followed with an increased majority.

A.N. went to Harrow School and played for the Harrow XI against Eton at Lord's. The *Manchester Guardian* recalled that the Prince and Princess of Wales and an unusually blue-blooded and brilliant assembly gathered around the ropes to watch. Hornby, described as 'a little fellow not much taller than his bat, opened the innings with Mr Charles Buller. Between them they set the foundation for a win and were carried shoulder high from pavilion to wicket and back again.'

It was at Harrow that he was first nicknamed 'Monkey' because of his short stature, his liveliness, or both. His sporting energy was certainly remarkable. On top of his cricket career, he played for England at rugby union in nine matches, some of them as captain, and turned out for Blackburn Rovers at football.

After Harrow he went on to Oxford but, according to his cricketing contemporary, Henry Leveson Gower, he was disappointed to find he had to study as well as play cricket. He returned to the family business and the life of a country gentleman, shooting and riding to hounds. By now, the family had moved to Shrewbridge Hall at Nantwich in Cheshire. He played county cricket for Cheshire and club matches for Blackburn, before starting with Lancashire.

He made his debut for the county playing at Whalley in 1867, opening the batting twice and scoring 2 and 3 runs in his first two knocks. He played for the county for 33 years, 17 of them as captain, from 1879–93 and 1897–98. In his early years he played in only six out of a possible 23 away matches, though he did make time for the more glamorous fixtures and three of these were in London. His front-foot batting style was dashing, hard-hitting and risk-taking – and the opposite of Barlow's. To put it positively, they were a perfect match. Hornby was also a superb fielder, swooping to stop a speeding ball with either hand.

His leadership was aggressive and inspirational, and while he was very much an amateur, he was supportive and protective of the professionals, regularly inviting them to his country house. He was also quick-tempered. In a match at Old Trafford, his son George dropped a catch. A spectator shouted, 'Oh dear, what will Pa say?' Hornby was straight off the pitch and into the crowd to put him right. He played his last game in 1899 at the age of 52, scoring 53 in his final innings.

Dick Barlow left school at 14 to work as an apprentice compositor in a printing office, then as an iron-moulder. In 1865 the family moved to Derbyshire when Dick's father got a job at the Staveley Ironworks. Dick played for the Ironworks' cricket club and for the club at Farsley in Leeds as a professional.

His break came in June 1871 when he was playing at Staveley against George Parr's All-England XI. A team-mate heard he was from Lancashire and advised him to get a trial in Manchester. He was given an hour's batting, half an hour's bowling and some fielding and catching and a few days later a letter arrived from the Lancashire committee inviting him to play against Yorkshire. He scored 28 not out in his first knock despite breaking a finger halfway through his innings, then took a wicket with his first ball in top-level cricket, helping Lancashire to a ten-wicket win.

Because of his place in *At Lord's*, Barlow is usually remembered as a batsman, and his batting was renowned for its obduracy. He claimed to have batted right through an innings 50 times and is even credited with being the origin of the term 'stonewalling'. In a match against Nottinghamshire in 1882 he scored 5 not out in two and a half hours while ten wickets fell at the other end. Legend has it that Bill Barnes, one of the Nottinghamshire bowlers, told him, 'Bowling at thee were like bowling at a stone wall.' Whether or not the source of the term was the American general, Thomas 'Stonewall' Jackson, who died in action in 1863, will probably never be known.

But Barlow was an all-rounder and the first player to open both the batting and the bowling in a Test match. He thought bowling was by far the more important skill. A colleague, Fred Root, later an England player, asked him if he should concentrate on batting or bowling. 'Bowl, bowl, bowl,' said Barlow, 'for goodness sake, bowl! Batsmen are like eggs in summer – eighteen a shilling. But bowlers, real bowlers, are as rare as a Lord's lunch to a professional cricketer when winter has set in.'

Kenneth Shenton, in his biography of Francis Thompson, calculates that Barlow took the wicket of W.G. Grace more times than any other bowler. W.G. was the first wicket of Barlow's first hat-trick, during the Gentlemen versus Players match at the Oval in 1884. In the same fixture three years later, he dismissed W.G., Alfred Lyttleton, Hornby, A.P. Lucas, A.G. Steel, A.H. Trevor and A.H. Evans, finishing with 7-55.

Francis Thompson: 'It is little I repair to the matches of the Southron folk'

Henry Newbolt at Clifton (centre right wearing hat): 'Play up and play the game' Picture courtesy of Clifton College

Clifton long ago. ' There's a breathless hush'. Picture courtesy of Clifton College

Cricket at Clifton. 'A bumping pitch and a blinding light' Picture courtesy of Clifton College

Clifton scorecard -- Collins 628 not out ! Picture courtesy of Clifton College

W.G. Grace – 'The long-whiskered Doctor, that laugheth the rules to scorn'. Picture courtesy of Clifton College

A.E.J. Collins, record-breaking schoolboy cricketer. Image reproduced courtesy of the Marylebone Cricket Club

Ranjitsinhji – 'A Light of the East'. Image reproduced courtesy of the Marylebone Cricket Club

A.N. 'Monkey' Hornby. Image reproduced courtesy of the Marylebone Cricket Club

Dick 'Stonewall' Barlow. Image reproduced courtesy of the Marylebone Cricket Club

The Battle of Abu Klea – 'The river of death has brimmed his banks'

Gloucestershire and the Graces: 'It's Glo'ster coming North, the irresistible'. Image reproduced courtesy of the Marylebone Cricket Club

Henry Newbolt: 'Capten, art tha sleepin' there below?' Picture courtesy of Clifton College

George Headley. Picture courtesy of Lancashire CCC

Learie Constantine. Image reproduced courtesy of the Marylebone Cricket Club

Sonny Ramadhin. Picture courtesy of Lancashire CCC

Alf Valentine. Picture courtesy of Lancashire CCC

West Indies

AF Rae c & b Jenkins	106	b Jenkins	24
JB Stollmeyer lbw b Wardle	20	b Jenkins	30
FMM Worrel b Bedser	52	c Doggart b Jenkins	45
ED Weekes b Bedser	63	run out	63
CL Walcott st Evans b Jenkins	14	not out	168
GE Gomez st Evans b Jenkins	1	c Edrich b Bedser	70
RJ Christiani b Bedser	33	not out	5
JDC Goddard b Wardle	14	c Evans b Jenkins	11
PEW Jones c Evans b Jenkins	0		
S Ramadhin not out	1		
AL Valentine c Hutton b Jenkins	5		
10b, 5lb, 1w, 1nb	17	8lb, 1nb	9
	326		**425-6**

Fall of wickets: 1-37, 2-128, 3-233, 4-262, 5-273, 6-27), 7-320, 8-320, 9-320, 10-326

Fall of wickets: 1-48, 2-75, 3-108, 4-146, 5-199, 6-410

England bowling	O	M	R	W	O	M	R	W
AV Bedser	40.0	14	60	3	44.0	16	80	1
WJ Edrich	16.0	4	30	0	13.0	2	37	0
RO Jenkins	35.2	6	116	5	59.0	13	174	4
JH Wardle	17.0	6	46	2	30.0	10	58	0
R Berry	19.0	7	45	0	32.0	15	67	0
NWD Yardley	4.0	1	12	0				

England

L Hutton st Walcott b Valentine	35	b Valentine	10
C Washbrook st Walcott b Ramadhin	36	b Ramadhin	114
WJ Edrich c Walcott b Ramadhin	8	c Jones b Ramadhin	8
GHG Doggart lbw b Ramadhin	0	b Ramadhin	25
WGA Parkhouse b Valentine	0	c Goddard b Valentine	48
NWD Yardley b Valentine	16	c Weekes b Valentine	19
TG Evans b Ramadhin	8	c Rae b Ramadhin	2
RO Jenkins c Walcott b Valentine	4	b Ramadhin	4
JH Wardle not out	33	lbw b Worrell	21
AV Bedser b Ramadhin	5	b Ramadhin	0
R Berry c Goddard b Jones	2	not out	0
2b, 1lb, 1w	4	16b, 7lb	23
	151		**274**

Fall of wickets: 1-62, 2-74, 3-74, 4-75, 5-86, 6-102, 7-110, 8-113, 9-122, 10-151

Fall of wickets: : 1-28, 2-57, 3-140, 4-218, 5-228, 6-238, 7-245, 8-248, 9-258, 10-274

West Indies bowling

	O	M	R	W	O	M	R	W
PEW Jones	8.4	2	13	1	7.0	1	22	0
FMM Worrell	10.0	4	20	0	22.3	9	39	1
AL Valentine	45.0	28	48	4	71.0	47	79	3
S Ramadhin	43.0	27	66	5	72.0	43	86	6
GE Gomez					13.0	1	25	0
JDC Goddard					6.0	6	0	0

Umpires: FS Lee, D Davies

Lancashire

AN Hornsby c JA Bush b W Grace.....	5	c Cranson b W Grace . 109
EG Barlow c W Grace b Miles.......	40	c and b Gilbert 25
AG Steeel c W Grace b Miles.........	0	c W Grace b Gilbert 6
DQ Steel c Gilbert by Miles...........	0	b EM Grace 22
VK Royle c Cranston by Miles.......	19	c JA Bush b Gilbert......19
WS Patterson c Gilbert b Miles.......	0	b Wright...............50
A Appleby c Gilbert b Miles..........	1	b EM Grace 7
EB Rowley b W Grace...............	8	b F Grace 0
A Watson c EM Grace b Miles........	3	not out 10
William McIntryre b W Grace	6	b EM Grace 8
R Pilling not out	0	c JA Bush b EM Grace 0
B1, w6...........................	7	B5, lb3, w6 14
	89	**262**

Gloucestershire

WG Grace c Watson b W McIntyre ...	32	not out 58
W Gilbert c Watson b AG Steel........	1	not out 10
W Midwinter lbw AG Steel	22	c Pilling b AG Steel.....25
Dr EM Grace st Pilling b AG Steel	21	b Appleby...............4
GF Grace c Watson b W McIntyre	7	st Pilling b AG Steel 6
J Cranston b W McIntyre.............	3	
CE Haynes run out	7	b AG Steel 12
EF Wright st Pilling b AG Steel........	4	b AG Steel 5
JA Bush not out	15	
A Robinson c Watson b W McIntyre ...	0	
RF Miles c Appleby b AG Steel	3	
B1.................................	1	B4, lb1.................5
	116	**125**

Umpires: Storer and CK Pullin

In his early days, Barlow played mostly in away fixtures because of the reluctance of amateurs like Hornby to travel. Only three of Barlow's first 13 matches were played at Old Trafford. Alec Watson, another professional, complained that Lancashire left Barlow out of some games because they did not want to pay him, preferring amateurs who could cover their own expenses.

Hornby and Barlow were respectively the irresistible force and the immovable object of Lancashire batting. They opened together for the first time in 1873 against Surrey at the Oval. For the first, but not the last time, Hornby ran Barlow out, this time before he had faced a ball. This was to become a regular event and Hornby would recompense his partner with a sovereign to make up for the possible bonus he had missed. The pair were unusually fast between the wickets. Hornby reckoned more runs were missed than were scored in county cricket. Barlow was not the only victim of Hornby's quick-single tendency. The great Nottinghamshire batsman, Arthur Shrewsbury, said he was sad when Hornby was dismissed, 'Otherwise he would have run everyone else out.'

Another milestone came two years later when the pair scored Lancashire's first-ever century opening partnership against Yorkshire at Old Trafford. Set a target of 146, they were sent out to open from their quarters at opposite ends of the pitch. They knocked off the runs between them, Hornby making 78 and Barlow 50. They ran off the field in opposite directions, Hornby to the pavilion, Barlow to his shed, but were surrounded by delirious crowds and carried shoulder high. Hornby was presented with a cane-handled bat by the Lancashire secretary and Barlow was rewarded with six sovereigns. The local papers went wild, the *City News* declaring, 'Such a sense of joyous triumph was surely never seen on a cricket ground.'

Hornby and Barlow both played at Test level home and away, but Barlow was far more successful. Hornby toured Australia once, in 1878/79, but without much success, his batting average sinking to 3.5 runs. In his debut Test at Sydney, he was dismissed twice by Fred 'The Demon' Spofforth.

Later in the tour, in February 1879, the same ground saw what became known as the Sydney riot. The England tourists were playing New South Wales and brought along an umpire, George Coulthard, from another state, Victoria. There was already rivalry, even hostility, between the two states, but things turned nasty when the star home batsman, Billy Murdoch, was given out by Coulthard. Home supporters stormed on to the pitch and attacked Coulthard and some of the England players. Some of the rioters were drunk, some were simply aggrieved by the umpire's decision, and some had wagered a lot of money on a New South Wales win. In the middle of the rumpus, Hornby, who had boxing on his long list of sports played, grabbed one rioter and marched him off to the pavilion. Play was abandoned and the game resumed after the Sunday rest day with the tourists winning by an innings.

Hornby fell to Spofforth again at the Oval in 1882. This was a one-off match, which Australia won by seven runs, inspiring the celebrated Ashes obituary in the *Sporting Times*: 'In affectionate remembrance of English Cricket, which died at the Oval on 29th August 1882. Deeply lamented by a large circle of sorrowing friends and acquaintances. R.I.P. The body will be cremated, and the ashes taken to Australia.' The story of the match is told in John Masefield's near-epic *Eighty-Five To Win*.

Hornby and Grace, with eighty-five to win,

Watched for some balls, then made

　　the runs begin.

Ten had gone up, when Hornby's wicket went

(His off stump), from a ball that Spofforth sent,

One, for fifteen, and Barlow took his place,

Barlow, our safest bat, came in with Grace.

Barlow, the wonder, famed in song and story,

The Red-Rose County's well-remembered glory,

The first ball Spofforth sent him

　　bowled him clean.

Two gone, of England's surest, for fifteen.

In 1884 Hornby captained England in the first Test match played at Old Trafford, opening the batting with W.G. Grace and getting stumped off the third ball he received. Barlow toured Australia three times and played in seven home Tests, including the 'Ashes' defeat in 1882, but

the following winter he was on the victorious tour
which reclaimed the Ashes, now in a real urn.
The lines of verse engraved on it concluded,

The great crowd will feel proud
Seeing Barlow and Bates coming home with
   the Urn, the Urn
And the rest coming home with the Urn.

One of Barlow's great performances was at Trent
Bridge in 1884, playing for the North of England
against Australia. He scored 10 not out and 102
and took 4-6 and 6-42. Spofforth had said before
the second innings, 'Give me the ball and they
won't get more than 60!' Barlow saw him off.

'Monkey' Hornby served as chairman of the
Lancashire club from 1878–98 and president from
1894 to 1916. Until the year before his death,
he visited Old Trafford regularly, arriving in an
invalid chair in his final years. He died in 1925,
six years after Barlow, at Parkfield near Nantwich

in Cheshire and was buried in the grounds of St Mary's Church in nearby Acton.

Barlow parted company with Lancashire in 1891 after being left out of the side for several matches and having a run-in with the committee. His last match, like his first, was against Yorkshire. He became a first-class umpire, and in the winter months a football referee, taking charge of the 1887 FA Cup tie at Deepdale between Preston North End and Hyde. Preston won 26-0, still a record for the competition.

Barlow was a modest man but proud of his cricketing accomplishments. He built his family a house in Blackpool with his initials carved in stone over the door and a stained-glass window with portraits of himself, Hornby, and another Lancastrian, Dick Pilling. He even designed his own headstone for his grave at Layton Cemetery, Blackpool. It depicted a ball passing through a wicket with the words 'Bowled at Last'. He also filled the rest of the stone, 'Here lie the remains of Richard Gorton Barlow, Died 31 July 1919, aged 68 years. For 21 seasons he was a playing member of the Lancashire County XI and for 21 years as an umpire in county matches. He also made three journeys to Australia with English teams. This is a consecutive record in first-class cricket which no other cricketer has achieved'. There was no room on the stone for anything more.

Chapter 11

ABU KLEA

The sand of the desert is sodden red,

Red with the wreck of a square that broke;

The Gatling's jammed and the Colonel dead,

And the regiment blind with dust and smoke.

The river of death has brimmed his banks,

And England's far, and Honour a name,

But the voice of a schoolboy rallies the ranks,

'Play up! play up! and play the game!'

THE BATTLE which Newbolt recounts in the second stanza of *Vitai Lampada* was fought on 17 January 1885 at Abu Klea, in the bend of the

137

River Nile, north of Khartoum. The combatants were the British Desert Column, made up of the Camel Corps and men from other regiments, and the forces of the Mahdi.

The previous year, an apprentice boat-builder, Mohammed Ahmed, had declared himself to be the Mahdi, or saviour, of the people of the Sudan. He led a revolt against the Khedive of Egypt, who ruled Sudan under the Ottoman Empire. The Khedive opted to withdraw his forces from their garrisons in Sudan and leave them to the Mahdi. At the suggestion of British Prime Minister William Gladstone, the Khedive appointed Charles Gordon, a former governor of the Sudan, to organise the withdrawal. The evacuation was difficult. The Nile was tough to navigate and in April the Mahdi captured Berber, a town on the Nile, cutting off Gordon's only land route to Egypt.

Messages from Khartoum to London and Cairo made it clear that the city could only hold out for 40 days, but Gordon would not leave. He sent his second-in-command, Colonel Stewart, with a message for Sir Evelyn Baring, the British high commissioner in Cairo, but Stewart was captured and killed by the Mahdists en route.

Gladstone was anxious not to get Britain further involved in the Sudan, but outraged public opinion, an intervention by Queen Victoria, and the threat of resignation from Secretary of State for War Lord Hartington, forced him to send an expeditionary force to rescue Gordon. The officer in charge of the rescue party, Lord Wolseley, had two options: the Nile, which would be slow, or overland, which would be risky. He chose the Nile for most of his force, but decided to form a Second Column which would try to reach Khartoum quickly overland.

Major General Herbert Stewart led the Desert Column, which comprised the Camel Corps and men from 21 other services. Some of the officers and men came from socially prestigious regiments, and an officer described the corps as 'London society on camels'. At the other end, the commanding officer of the 2nd Life Guards assigned his regiment's drunks to the corps on the grounds that they would struggle to find alcohol in the desert. The chosen regimental march was the Scottish air, *The Campbells are Coming*, which inevitably became 'the camels are coming'.

The officers included Colonel Fred Burnaby. Burnaby was popular within his regiment, the Royal Horse Guards, but was disliked by the royal family and his own commander, the Duke of Cambridge, who were annoyed by his disrespectful jokes about them. He was also a Member of Parliament, a journalist, and a cross-Channel balloonist.

The Desert Column began its march to Khartoum on 30 December 1884. By sunset on

16 January 1885, they were close to the wells at Abu Klea. They had left their last water source 43 miles back, but their scouts reported a large force of Mahdists ahead. Stewart decided against a night attack on the Wadi and built a defensive position two miles short of their target.

At daylight on the 17th, Stewart formed his men into a square and they advanced towards the wells. Suddenly the square was ambushed by a large Mahdist force around 3,000 strong, hiding in the Wadi. In the fighting that followed, a gap opened in the square as the one Gardner machine gun was moved to provide cover fire and the men were ordered to wheel out of the square to protect it. The gun fired 70 rounds, then jammed, and the crew were rushed by Mahdists. Several Mahdists broke into the square but found themselves trapped by a crowd of camels. The British forces surrounded and opened fire on the Mahdists inside the square, and the battle was over in less than a quarter of an hour, the 19th Hussars moving forward to seize the wells.

Some 1,100 Mahdists were killed and the British lost nine officers and 65 other ranks. Among the dead was Colonel Burnaby, killed by a spear to the throat. On the afternoon of the 18th, the column continued its advance to Khartoum. After a series of skirmishes, it reached its destination on 28 January. It was two days too late to save Gordon. He had been killed on the steps of his palace when the Mahdi's forces took Khartoum on the 26th. The British withdrew from Sudan, leaving the Mahdists to rule for 13 years. In Britain, Gordon was hailed as a national hero, and within two months Gladstone had left Downing Street.

Newbolt stretched his poetic licence. Most of the blood which reddened the desert sands was that of the Mahdi's men, not the Desert Column. The British square was temporarily broken, not wrecked. The machine gun did jam, but it was

the American Gardner, not a Gatling. But at least
Newbolt had the poetic advantage over William
McGonagall, whose account of the battle relied
as always on robust rhyming.

Ye sons of Mars, come join with me,
And sing in praise of Sir Herbert
   Stewart's little army,
That made ten thousand Arabs flee
At the charge of the bayonet at Abu Klea.

Eighteen stanzas follow recounting the battle.

Then General Stewart took up a good
   position on a slope,
Where he guessed the enemy could not
   with him cope,
Where he knew the rebels must advance,
All up hill and upon open ground, which was
   his only chance.

As for Fred Burnaby:

Oh! it was an exciting and terrible sight,

To see Colonel Burnaby engaged in the fight:

With sword in hand, fighting with

   might and main,

Until killed by a spear-thrust in the jugular vein.

Chapter 12

A LIGHT OF THE EAST

I sing a glorious hero bold, his name well
known to fame,
A man of might in friendly fight, in our fine old
English game;
A Prince of our Indian Empire, the willow he
wields with ease,
And with practised skill and right good will, he
scores his centuries.

IN 1897 Queen Victoria celebrated the 60th
anniversary of her accession to the throne. For
Francis Thompson, the jubilee year was the

apogee of the British Empire and of the game of cricket. 'The art of preparing consummate wickets – wickets which make batting an ease and a delight, bowling a game of patience and endurance – has reached its height.' As Thompson described, a brilliantly sunny summer had done such wickets full justice, and a wonderful fertility of consummate batsmen had taken full advantage of the wickets and the weather. Yet, he argued, the most successful bowlers were Tom Richardson, Arthur Mold and Charles Kortright – all three fast men.

Like Henry Newbolt, Thompson was not much of a cricketer. The fastest bowling he ever faced may have been from his sisters at Colwyn Bay. But unlike Newbolt, he was a keen student of the game who left behind piles of newspaper cuttings reporting great matches over the years. His cricket poetry may have been romantic and nostalgic, but some of his prose was thoroughly detailed and practical, particularly in a review he wrote of a book by the great Indian batsman K.S. Ranjitsinhji. *The Jubilee Book of Cricket* was published in 1897, and the author proudly declared that it was 'dedicated by her gracious permission to Her Majesty the Queen-Emperor'.

Thompson's review is entitled *A Prince of India on the Prince of Games*. Ranjitsinhji was not in fact the prince of anywhere at this time, though he was to take on the title in his home state a few years later after decades of intrigue. Ranjitsinhji was born on 10 September 1872 to his father, a farmer, and one of his wives. His childhood home was in the village of Sadodar in the western province of Nawanagar and his family were distantly related to Vibhaji, the Jam Sahib of the region. These years at Vibhaji's court are unclear and contested, but in 1876 a son was born to him, named Kalubha, and he became heir to the throne. However, he was to be notorious for violence and depravity, including multiple rapes and an alleged attempt to poison his father. Vibhaji disinherited him and looked for another heir from a branch of the family. His first choice died within a year of being selected and Ranji became heir in 1878. But it's unclear whether Vibhaji ever formally adopted him, and Ranjitsinhji's prospects appeared to evaporate when a woman at Vibhaji's court gave birth to a son.

But Vibhaji still supported him financially and sent him to Rajkumar College in Bombay, where he won a gold medal for English-speaking at the age of 14, by reciting *Young Lochinvar*. In 1888 the college principal, Chester MacNaghten, took him and two other boys to London. One of the early treats was a visit to the Oval to watch Surrey take on the Australian tourists, a day which helped shift his enthusiasm from tennis to cricket. He failed the preliminary entrance exams to Trinity College, Cambridge, but was taken on as a 'youth of position'. He had hopes to get a Blue at tennis, but after watching the Australians and playing some friendly matches while on holiday in Bournemouth, he decided to make cricket his game. The basic principle of batting in those days was to hit the ball back where it came from. It was his coach at Cambridge, Daniel Hayward, who experimented with fixing Ranjitsinhji's right leg to the ground while leaving his left leg free. He found that by moving his front leg to the right, he could play a leg glance, a shot which was to be part of his legend. As his Cambridge career progressed he was awarded a Blue and played for a team of Oxford and Cambridge men, past and present, against the Australians. It was around this time that he was given the nickname Ranji, which was to stay with him for life. He was also becoming a snappy dresser and lavish entertainer, which brought on the financial problems which burdened him for the rest of his life.

An early acquaintance was another young man from Rajkot, Mohandas Karamchand Gandhi. Another friendship, with Hayward's cricketing son Tom, might have helped him to join Surrey, but he opted for a then weaker side, Sussex, partly because of his friendship with C.B. Fry and the Sussex skipper, the Australian Billy Murdoch. It's also possible he thought it would guarantee him a regular place in the team. He may also have been given a deal offered to amateurs because of his financial problems.

His career at Sussex took off in 1895 with a debut appearance against MCC in which he scored 77 not out in his first innings, then made his maiden century in the second innings with 150 in 155 minutes. His reputation blossomed, thanks in part to his revolutionary leg glance, and the following year he was knocking on the Test match door. As a warm-up he turned out for the Gentlemen against the Players at Lord's, scoring

47 and 51 not out, off a star quartet of pacemen, Tom Richardson, George Lohmann, JT Hearne and Johnny Briggs.

At this time, the England side was selected by the ground who were hosting the match. He was overlooked for the first Test at Lord's by MCC and its head Lord Harris, a former governor of Bombay, possibly because of his Indian heritage. The second Test was at Old Trafford and the Lancashire skipper Monkey Hornby invited him to play. Ranjitsinhji said he could not take part without the agreement of the Australians. Their skipper Harry Trott was delighted so Ranjitsinhji played, scoring a careful 62 in his first innings and making a maiden Test century, 154 not out, in the second.

The crowd were ecstatic, and Ranjitsinhji's reputation grew. However, there was also an element of racism among the MCC membership. A journalist, Home Gordon, reported that he praised Ranjitsinhji in conversation with a member, only to be told he should be expelled from MCC for 'having the disgusting degeneracy to praise a dirty black'. Some MCC members were reported as complaining of 'a n***er showing us how to play the game of cricket'. But *Wisden* summed up the popular view: 'The famous young Indian fairly rose to the occasion, playing an innings that could, without exaggeration, be fairly described as marvellous.' That year, the songwriter Charles T. West composed the chorus:

Ran-jit-sinh-ji,
All the way from Inji.
Right well he plays, and earns our praise,
Ranji Ranjitsinhji.
'Cuts' for three, and 'smacks' for four,
Soon to the century mounts his score,
And loud the crowd then shout and roar
Bravo! Bravo! Ranji!

Ranjitsinhji was establishing himself as the second-greatest batsman after W.G. Grace and the first for style and elegance. In 1899 he took over as captain of Sussex and led the side to fifth place in the Championship, its highest position to that date. By now some opponents tried to block his leg glances by putting more fielders on the leg side, but he responded by driving more. As he matured, he grew stouter, and his batting became sturdier and less elegant. He had some thin seasons, but by 1904 he was topping the averages again with 2,077 runs at 74.17.

An exploration of Ranjitsinhji's genius was offered by G.W. Beldam and C.B. Fry in their 1907 book *Great Batsmen – their Methods at a Glance.* They said he was usually described as a genius with very unorthodox methods or buried under a heap of vague epithets of wonder. Their explanation is that he was more subtle in his joints, especially the wrists, than anyone else in the game, and was appreciably quicker. And he allowed the ball to get much closer to him than most batsmen. He may have let it come only a foot closer but that foot made all the difference.

Between seasons Ranjitsinhji returned to India to fight for the throne of Nawanagar, travelling round the country to drum up popular support and lobbying senior British officials including the Viceroy Lord Elgin and his successor Lord Curzon. There were rumours of assassination plots involving Ranjitsinhji or aimed at him. His manoeuvring finally succeeded and he was installed as Jam Sahib on 11 March 1907, remaining there for two decades.

His visits to Britain became rarer, but his last cricket appearances were not until 1920, when he played in three first-class matches despite having lost an eye in a shooting accident while hunting grouse on the North Yorkshire Moors near Langdale End. He retired after scoring

24,692 runs at an average of 56.37. He died of heart failure on 2 April 1933 after a short illness. His ashes were scattered over the river Ganges.

Ranjitsinhji's finances had been in dire straits for much of his life and money was one of the driving forces behind the *Jubilee Book* which he worked on with Fry and other friends, dictating to a shorthand writer as he went along. The book was warmly received and financially successful. The first half of the book is down to earth, 'A good night's rest and a perfect digestion are the chief foundations of success in cricket.' Ranjitsinhji argues that cricket implies a certain amount of physical capacity and cricket pitches are a pretty good test of physique. And he quotes W.G. Grace, 'Temperance in food and drink, regular sleep and exercise I have laid down as a golden rule.'

Ranjitsinhji's detailed guide on how to play the game begins, surprisingly, with fielding, as a mild protest against the prominence given to batting and bowling. He says fielding was much neglected at the public schools, more at the universities, and more still at county level. As for club cricket, fielding was regarded as a necessary evil which must be tolerated because without it batting and bowling would be impossible. Yet for winning matches, fielding was nearly as important as bowling and batting. Thompson agreed, and recalled an old Lancashire hero, the Reverend Vernon Royle. '[He was] a pretty and stylish bat, but a wonderful fielder who routinely swooped and stopped balls which team-mates would have let pass and hurled it back from square to hit a single stump.' Thompson recalls an Australian playing against Lancashire, hitting the ball past cover point and looking for a run. 'No, no,' said his partner. 'The policeman is there.'

Ranjitsinhji analyses all fielding positions from point and cover point round to short leg.

'Wicketkeeping is the most difficult and the most important fielding position, while long stop is already becoming a rarity as wickets get better and byes don't get past the keeper as regularly.'

Bowling, says Ranjitsinhji, is an art. Or rather, bowling well is an art. 'After learning to bowl straight and acquiring some stamina, the bowler must learn the next and most important secret of his art – a perfect command of length.' He says that 'with good wickets being now almost universal, mere pace and attempts at break are rendered more or less harmless, but the bowler who can keep up his length is sure to have his reward sooner or later'. He believes 'it is head work and the study of the batsman's peculiarities which puts the crown on a bowler'. There are some bowlers who seem to fascinate the batsman and make him do what they want in spite of himself.

Some of Ranjitsinhji's sternest words are directed at one of the game's most familiar

characters at all levels and over the centuries –
the grumpy bowler. He believes nothing is more
upsetting for an entire team than a bowler who
loses his temper or sulks. 'There are various signs
of a sulky bowler, he takes a long time to get to
his place in the field when he's not bowling; after
fielding the ball he throws it back needlessly hard
to the detriment of someone's hands; if he misses
the ball, he is reluctant to run after it. Often, he
bowls too fast or too short and generally gives the
impression he doesn't care. Bowling misfortunes
often test a man's temper, but he must keep
complete control over himself. He is playing for
his side, not for himself, and when everyone in a
team fosters a spirit of mutual cohesion, it is a joy
to itself and all the world besides.'

Ranjitsinhji is also concerned with what he
calls 'Captain's Bowlomania' – a captain who
bowls either too much or too little. He believes
'we all know, especially in club cricket, a captain

who comes on to bowl at one end and remains a fixture, all the changes coming at the other end. This Bowlomania is absolutely fatal in a captain and very difficult to cure.'

Thompson does take issue with Ranjitsinhji on the issue of under-arm bowling. In the early centuries of the game, bowlers skidded the ball along the ground as if they were playing bowls, and cricket bats were more like hockey sticks. In the 1760s, when bowlers began to pitch the ball through the air, straight bats took over. Round-arm bowling spread in the first half of the 19th century and shared with under-arm until over-arm began in the 1860s. By the end of the 19th century, under-arm was a rarity, except when an injured bowler needed to complete an over, or a bowler convicted of no-balling went under-arm to finish it off.

Nearly a century later, in 1981, uproar broke out at the Benson & Hedges World Series Final at the Melbourne Cricket Ground when the Australian bowler Trevor Chappell was ordered by his captain and brother, Greg, to roll the final ball along the ground to prevent the New Zealand batsman Brian McKechnie from hitting it for six to tie the match. Thompson argues that an under-arm bowler can pitch every ball up with ease, while over-armers find it hard work. Furthermore, a pitched-up over-arm ball will come right on to the bat. An under-arm ball will drop suddenly and a batsman who tries to clout it may play over it. If he plays back, it's difficult to get the ball away. Also, yorkers are easier for the under-armer because they put less strain on the weaker arm.

Batting is for Ranjitsinhji the most fascinating and delightful part of cricket. He warns that the impulse of every beginner is to draw back when the ball is coming at him. He does this by moving his right leg backwards in the direction of short leg. 'This is a mistake. He should keep his back foot firmly in place.' Ranjitsinhji catalogues the whole range of strokes, the cuts – late, square and forward; the drives – off, straight and on; the pull and the hook. He goes into great detail on all of them. including the back glide, a stroke no longer heard of. He says the simplest way to play it is to step a little towards the wicket with the right foot, then quickly draw the left foot up to it, turn to face the ball, and play the shot with a half push, half turn of the bat. He plays it in a different way himself, stepping across the wicket with the left foot, putting the bat in front of the right leg, and pivoting on his right toe to play the ball on the on side. But, he says, don't play this way if it doesn't come naturally.

The *Jubilee Book* even contains advice for umpires. 'They can be chary of no-balling bowlers but will almost invariably give a batsman run out or stumped, even when his foot is on the line.'

He doesn't see why umpires should not be strict with bowlers who drag their foot over the crease.

Francis Thompson thought the modern enthusiasm for the game exemplified by Ranjitsinhji did not compare with that of previous generations. He recalls the account by a clergyman, the Reverend John Mitford, of a visit to the home of Billy Beldam, the elderly veteran of Hambledon and Surrey. 'In his kitchen, black with age, hangs the trophy of his victories, the delight of his youth, the exercise of his manhood, and the glory of his age – his bat. Reader, believe me when I tell you, I trembled when I touched it. It seemed an act of profaneness, of violation. I pressed it to my lips and returned it to its sanctuary.' Thompson concludes, 'Let that fine bit of rhodomontade put you in tune for approaching the best analysis of cricket yet produced by a magnificent cricketer.' A warm tribute, but not as poetic as the prose of the celebrated cricket writer Neville Cardus, 'When Ranjitsinhji batted, a strange light was seen for the first time on English fields, a light of the East.'

Chapter 13

GLO'STER COMING NORTH

This day of seventy-eight they are come up
    north against thee
This day of seventy-eight long ago!
The champion of the centuries, he cometh up
    against thee,
With his brethren, every one a famous foe!
The long-whiskered Doctor that laugheth the
    rules to scorn,
While the bowler, pitched against him, bans the
    day he was born;
And G.F. with his science makes the fairest
    length forlorn;
They are come from the West to work thee woe!

THE *MANCHESTER Guardian* was ecstatic.
'For once Manchester appeared to have forgotten
that Cotton was king and gave up to the
fascination of our national game with unrestrained
enthusiasm. All classes of the community were
represented, and a good hit or clever bit of fielding
never failed of its appropriate reward in the cheer
of the occupants of the pavilion or the delighted
shouts from the lower benches.'

Lancashire had been snubbed by
Gloucestershire for a decade and a half, and
it may have been the camaraderie of Hornby
and W.G. Grace which finally clinched the
fixture. Gloucestershire were still the giants,
but Lancashire went into the match with
some confidence after wins over Yorkshire
and Nottinghamshire. The teams and
their supporters arrived at Old Trafford on
Thursday, 25 July 1878, only to find it had
been raining. The overnight storm had left

the wicket dead and there was more rain on
the way.

The team sheets read:

Lancashire: Mr A.N. Hornby, R.G.
Barlow, Mr A.G. Steel, Mr D.Q. Steel,
Mr V. Royle, Mr A. Appleby, Mr W.S.
Patterson, Mr E.B. Rowley, A. Watson,
W. McIntyre, R. Pilling.

Gloucestershire: Mr G.F. Grace, Mr E.V.
Wright, W. Midwinter, Mr C. Haynes,
Dr E.M. Grace, Mr W.G. Grace, Mr
Gilbert, Mr J.A. Cranston, Mr J.A. Bush,
Mr A. Robinson, Mr R.F. Miles.

The misters were of course amateurs,
the non-misters the professionals. The
distinction continued until 1962, when the last
Gentlemen versus Players match was played at
Scarborough. The following year MCC finally

abandoned the fixture, 157 years after the first contest.

Play began at 12.30. Lancashire's skipper Edmund Rowley won the toss and chose to bat despite the sodden ground, the bad light and the threatening storm, and Hornby and Barlow opened, facing W.G. Grace and Miles. Hornby began with a four, then a single but was caught behind in Grace's second over. The Steel brothers both went for a duck, before the rain returned with the score at 18/3.

Play did not resume till nearly 4pm, despite growing impatience in the crowd. Royle made some quick runs off Grace but was caught in the slips off Miles for 19. Appleby and Patterson both went cheaply, but Barlow was still there with stubborn defence interspersed with some big hitting. He and Rowley held things together until the rain came down again briefly. On the resumption Rowley, Watson and McIntyre all went quickly, and play ended with Lancashire on 88/9 and Barlow still there on 40 not out.

Day two began with bright sunshine and a festival feel. By the close of play some 10,000 spectators had come along compared with around 2,000 on day one. Barlow and the wicketkeeper Dick Pilling resumed the innings but after one wide ball Barlow was caught at mid-off, leaving Lancashire all out for 89, with Barlow first man in and last man out for 40.

G.F. (Fred) Grace and Wright opened the batting for Gloucestershire but both went quickly, and Haynes was run out for 7. W.G. Grace and Midwinter calmed things down and took the score to 42 before Midwinter fell lbw to Gill for 22. E.M. Grace and W.G. pulled the innings together for a while. W.G. was looking settled and reached 32 before a ball from McIntyre rose sharply and was clipped to Watson at slip. E.M. charged down the wicket repeatedly at A.G. Steel but was eventually beaten by turn and stumped by Pilling for 21. The tailenders went quickly, leaving Gloucestershire all out for 116, a relief for Lancashire who had feared they might be chasing 200. McIntyre, bowling with pace and accuracy, took four of the wickets. A.G. Steel took four more.

Shortly before 5pm Hornby and Barlow opened again and from the start Hornby was at his most dazzling, driving with power and keeping the ball down. W.G. threw seven bowlers at him – himself, Miles, Haynes, Wright, Midwinter, Gilbert and E.M. Grace, but Hornby was not troubled. At the other end, Barlow was his usual safe and sober self and by the close at 6.30pm Lancashire had reached 90 for no wicket, with Hornby on 68 not out and Barlow on 16.

The third day on Saturday saw the largest crowd to date watch cricket at Old Trafford. *Wisden* quoted a correspondent known mysteriously as 'one who ought to know all about it' reporting that 16,000 spectators turned out, so four entrances had to be opened. Even that did not give enough quick access and some 2,000 went round and climbed over the boards on to the ground without paying. The total number of spectators over the three days was more than 28,000 and the takings at the gate were huge: Thursday £88 7s; Friday £269 5s; Saturday £400 5s.

The final day's play started promptly at noon with Hornby and Barlow facing Gilbert and Miles. Hornby scored three from Gilbert's first delivery and the total quickly passed 100. But at 106, Barlow was caught and bowled by Gilbert for 26. Hornby reached his hundred but was caught at cover point off the next ball. D.Q. Steel made 22 and Royle 19, but the biggest contributor after Hornby was Patterson. His innings nearly came to a premature end when he drove the ball to the boundary, where a spectator on a bench stopped it and the fielder, Cranston, dragged it back with his foot. The crowd shouted 'four' so the batsmen stopped running. Cranston returned the ball, and the wicket was broken. The umpire didn't hear the shout and Patterson was given run out. Lancashire objected and the crowd shouted, 'No, no, no' and 'a four'. The two captains argued for a time until E.M. Grace, a coroner by profession, strode to the boundary and conducted an inquest with the crowd. Patterson was called back and went on to reach 50. The innings ended at 4.10pm with Lancashire all out for 262.

Gloucestershire came out to bat for the last time at 4.45pm. They needed 236 runs to win, which meant they had no chance but a real danger of defeat. The crowd was now enormous and was spilling on to the pitch. There were hopes that W.G. would open the batting but in the event G.F. and Wright opened. Wickets fell steadily. Wright was caught and bowled by A.G. Steel for 5. Fred Grace was stumped by Pilling for 6 and Haynes was run out for 7. Midwinter held the innings together for a while but was caught behind by Pilling for 25 with the score at 43 and E.M. Grace followed at 52. The fifth wicket of Haynes went with the score at 56. But W.G. and Gilbert took control and saw the day out. W.G. was at the top of his game, scoring eight boundaries, one of them soaring over the heads of the crowd. At the close, Gloucestershire were 125/5, 111 runs short of victory, with W.G. 58 not out and Gilbert unbeaten on 10.

The *Manchester Guardian* declared that the match had greatly enhanced the reputation of the Lancashire team. It thought they had started badly because of skipper Rowley's decision to take the first knock but had completely retrieved the situation in the second innings. It was convinced that, had time allowed, Lancashire would have won despite the 'super excellence' of W.G. and

Gilbert. The following year, 1879, Lancashire were declared joint county champions with Nottinghamshire, and two years later in 1881 they were champions outright.

Chapter 14

THE SHADOWY COAST

IT WAS while he was at the monastery at Pantasaph that Francis Thompson tried to reach a reconciliation with his father. In 1893 he heard he was at Rhyl so went to see him but found he had left the week before.

In April 1896 he heard that his father was dying. He went up to Ashton but was too late. His father had died the night before. He did see one of his sisters 'looking the merest girl still, and sweeter than ever. She did not look a day older than ten years ago. She said I looked very changed and worn.'

Thompson stayed at Pantasaph for four years. It was on a visit to London in 1896 that he fell in love for the last time, with Katherine Douglas King, a writer of short stories who he met at the Meynells' house. But Katie's family, supported by the Meynells, thwarted any attempted courtship, and when Thompson next visited London he found Katie had married. His agonies were aggravated by the death of one of his few close male friends, Coventry Patmore, his soulmate in theology, poetry and mysticism.

The final decade of Thompson's life was a descent into physical and psychological deterioration. His first volume of poems had been well received, but the next two had a mixed reception and did not sell well. One critic called the work 'a dictionary of obsolete English suffering from a fierce fit of delirium tremens'. Some were more enthusiastic. Oscar Wilde asked, 'Why can't I write poetry like that?'

By 1900 he was taking up to five ounces of laudanum a day. He was still turning out around 50 articles a year on literature, politics and cricket, and was earning a decent living, but his behaviour was increasingly despondent, erratic and solitary. Everard Meynell recalls the account of one of Thompson's landladies. 'It's very nice for Mr Thompson; he's got the trains at his back every half hour and more when he's in his bedroom. But then the trains, when all's said and done, aren't the same as the company he could get downstairs.' A friend, Wilfred Whitten, met Thompson for a rare restaurant dinner, 'The tragedy of his aspect was obvious. Of the glorious moments he must have lived in when the soul was master, very few external traces could be seen, save his eyes.'

In August 1906 his condition was so dire that Meynell dispatched him to a Franciscan monastery at Crawley in Sussex. He recovered a little despite taking laudanum sent him by a druggist in London. He returned to the capital and continued to write, but it's no surprise that in July 1907 he stayed away from Lancashire's match against Middlesex at Lord's, a step which was to be the starting point of his great poem.

Meynell arranged another stay away from London, this time at the Sussex home of another literary friend, Wilfred Scawen Blunt. Blunt was soon to warn Meynell that Thompson was near to death. In October he returned to London and a month later he was admitted to hospital and registered as suffering from morphomania, or opium addiction. He died at dawn on 13 November 1907 aged 47 years and 11 months. At death he weighed only 70lb (5 stone). Laudanum had been the cause of his weakened state, but the doctors said that tuberculosis had destroyed one of his lungs and the laudanum might have extended his life a little. He left behind poems and unopened letters, tobacco pipes too old for smoking, a broken lamp, and pens which could not write.

His funeral was thinly attended with just a dozen mourners and some tributes were less than kind. An American professor dismissed him as 'the poet of sin' but the literary world was warm in its tributes. George Meredith hailed him as, 'A true poet, one of the small band.' Another giant, G.K. Chesterton, himself a convert to Catholicism, called him 'a shy volcano' and wrote, 'We lost the greatest poetic energy since Browning.' Years later J.R.R. Tolkien wrote that Thompson's work had been a major influence on his own. His gravestone at St Mary's Roman Catholic Cemetery in Kensal Green, west London, bore a line from a poem he wrote for his godson, a Meynell, 'Look for me in the nurseries of Heaven.'

Chapter 15

AN ISLANDER'S WAR

NEWBOLT WAS virulent in his feelings about the Germans, who he saw as 'Godless barbarians'. He decided that at the age of 47 he was too old to enlist, though some friends of his generation did sign up. His son Frank enlisted as a second lieutenant in the Oxfordshire and Cambridgeshire Light Infantry. Newbolt's contribution was to be propaganda. He toured the country delivering lectures on 'Poetry and Patriotism'. Audiences could be as high as a thousand or just a handful 'mostly knitting', and he was unenthusiastic about some of the people who put him up on his travels.

One host, in Newcastle, was 'decidedly middle class' and the maid talked to Newbolt 'as an equal'. Newbolt had made clear his views on conflict a decade earlier during the Boer War in an exchange with Rudyard Kipling. Kipling had returned home from South Africa and posted in *The Times* a poem called *The Islanders,* bitterly critical of the public-school generals who he believed were making a mess of the British campaign. Newbolt's response was to defend chivalry, which he believed was part of the British view of war: 'War is either a game or else a brutality worse than bestial. The Islander, the child of all ages upon our playing fields, will "play the game", he will win if he can do it within the rules but not at the cost of that which is more than any game.' At the end of 1914 Newbolt's knighthood was announced in the New Year's Honours list. For the ceremony he insisted on wearing knee-breeches and ruffles in the style of a century before.

In 1915 Frank went to France but was only there for three weeks. During the second Battle of Ypres he was ordered to take his men to occupy some farm buildings. They were shelled through the night. At dawn a bullet hit Frank's knapsack and knocked him over, then a shell blew him into the branches of an apple tree. The next thing he knew he was on a hospital train in England suffering from severe shell shock. He convalesced, while Newbolt complained, 'I'm sorry he isn't doing more for his country.' At least Frank survived, unlike the sons of a number of Newbolt's friends.

The nearest Newbolt himself came to the fighting was during a German air raid on London while he was hosting a dinner. The guests fled and a bomb shook the building. It had landed down the street near the Chelsea Pensioners' Hospital, destroying another house and killing everyone in it. Back at the family home at Netherhampton in Wiltshire he saw an ambulance carrying wounded officers. He observed, 'A gruesome sight but wonderful to think that they were probably fighting only two days ago.'

One of the consolations for Newbolt and Margaret was the birth of Celia's daughter, Barbara, better known as Jill. A son, Patrick, was to follow three years later. By now Newbolt had found himself a part-time role doing propaganda for the Admiralty. He also experimented with food shopping to observe the new rationing system in action, but was annoyed by 'lady customers who hadn't thought of their purchases beforehand and took up time by long and very stupid conversations over the counter'.

By October 1918, Newbolt had inside information that a German surrender was close and on 11 November he celebrated the Armistice in his office hearing cheering crowds on Fleet Street and The Strand.

Chapter 16

NEWBOLT AND COMPANY

NEWBOLT NOW decided it was time to leave the law, and he gave up his chambers without quitting the Bar. In 1900, his publisher, John Murray, invited him to edit a literary magazine, the *Monthly Review*, and Newbolt brought Ella into the team. She had recently moved in with the Newbolts when they moved to a new, larger house a few streets from their old home.

Newbolt's circle of literary and artistic friends was expanding, thanks in part to the Vienna Cafe in New Oxford Street, where the regulars included John Masefield and the painter Walter

Sickert. Another new name was added when Emma showed him a collection of poems by an anonymous writer, calling himself W.R. This was Walter de la Mare, a clerk in the offices of the Standard Oil Company and the author of poems of dreams, fantasy and fairies. De la Mare finally turned up in person at the *Monthly Review* offices on Albemarle Street and a 30-year friendship began.

Emma was smitten by De la Mare and helped him organise his work for publication. Newbolt helped the young poet and his family financially and secured him support from the Royal Bounty, a fund supplying money to the female relatives of army officers who died of their wounds, but which also supported artists and writers. He helped De la Mare select work for his first volume of adult verse, *Poems 1906*, though the poet's reputation was not finally established until 1910 with publication of *The Listeners*:

'Is there anybody there?' said the Traveller,

Knocking on the moonlit door;

And his horse in the silence champed the grasses

Of the forest's ferny floor...

Newbolt's circle was now to include two of the greatest novelists of the age. Thomas Hardy's historical drama *The Dynasts*, set during the Napoleonic Wars, had a mostly unflattering critical response. Newbolt's was one of the few favourable reviews and the two kept in touch for many years after.

Newbolt first met Joseph Conrad at the Savile Club on Piccadilly at a Saturday afternoon symposium of half a dozen writers and artists. He had been a reader of the Polish writer's novels and short stories. *The Nigger of the Narcissus* had repelled him, but *Lord Jim* had won him over. The man himself did not disappoint Newbolt, with an aquiline and commanding profile but with intellectual and calm features, 'Then came a sharp surprise. As we sat in our little half-circle round the fire, and talked on anything and everything, I saw a third Conrad emerge – an artistic self, sensitive and restless to the last degree. The more he talked, the more quickly he consumed his cigarettes, rolling them so fast one after another that the fingers of both hands were stained a deep yellow almost as far as the palms.' Conrad was also struggling financially, and Newbolt helped him secure £500 from the Bounty, though Conrad was very truculent about how the payment was arranged, demanding half of it to pay outstanding bills.

H.G. Wells burst on to the literary scene in 1895 with the publication of *The Time Machine*. Seven years later, Newbolt wrote an enthusiastic review of his new novel, *The Sea Lady*. Wells invited him to join the Co-Efficients, a dining club for politicians like the future prime minister,

Arthur Balfour, and thinkers like the young Bertrand Russell. Wells and Newbolt started an unlikely friendship and walked and talked together. In the end, Newbolt found Wells's views too radical. Given his own domestic arrangements, he could hardly complain about Wells's views on free love, but he did strongly reject his political philosophy. At least, Newbolt said, one could argue with Wells, unlike George Bernard Shaw. 'Arguing with GBS was like arguing with a Jack-in-a-Box.'

Newbolt was now turning into a country gentleman, taking over a house at Northallerton in North Yorkshire, then at Netherhampton near Salisbury in Wiltshire. But there was strain and distress in his family. His sister Milly died on 17 August 1903. She had been ill for four years but collapsed suddenly while on holiday at Southwold on the Suffolk coast. Her death certificate gave the cause as a brain haemorrhage, but it may have been a heart attack. Margaret and Ella were also going through a difficult time, both mentally and physically.

In 1905 Newbolt wrote a book about the Battle of Trafalgar to celebrate the 100th anniversary. Much of it was drawn from the letters of his grandfather, Charles Newbolt, whose frigate had been at Trafalgar but did not take part in the battle. Newbolt's book led to an argument about the tactics deployed by the admirals Nelson and Collingwood. At the end of the narrative, he added five of his naval poems including Drake's Drum, which were set to music by Charles Stanford and added to Sir Henry Wood's Promenade Concert for the Nelson celebration that year.

The Great War began in the first week of August 1914. On 2 August, Germany occupied Luxembourg, and on the 3rd, it declared war on France; on the same day it sent the Belgian government an ultimatum demanding unimpeded right of way through any part of Belgium. The Belgians refused, and early on the morning of the 4th the Germans invaded. King Albert ordered his forces to resist and called for support under the 1839 Treaty of London. Britain demanded Germany comply with the Treaty and respect Belgian neutrality. The German reply was deemed unsatisfactory, and that evening Britain declared war on Germany.

Chapter 17

THE RIPPER

WHILE MUCH of Francis Thompson's work is profoundly spiritual, other poems suggest a much darker side. Some lines, particularly in *Poems on Children*, feel rather queasy these days and have led to charges of paedophiliac tendencies similar to those levelled at Charles Dodgson, whose pen name was, of course, Lewis Carroll. Some blood-curdling poems have been quoted to add him to the list of suspects in perhaps the most notorious murder case in British history.

The Jack the Ripper murders were committed between 31 August and 9 November 1888, in and around the district of Whitechapel in east London. Whitechapel was a crowded, squalid area, home to around 80,000 people, many of them immigrants including Jewish refugees fleeing persecution in Russia, Germany and Poland. Prostitution was rife – the police estimated there were 1,200 prostitutes and 62 brothels in the neighbourhood. Housing was grim, and over half of the children born there died before they were five years old.

The five Ripper victims were Mary Ann Nichols, Annie Chapman, Elizabeth Stride, Catherine Eddowes and Mary Jane Kelly. All were found with their throats slashed, their abdomens cut open and, in at least three cases, internal organs removed. There were 11 more murders in Whitechapel and surrounding areas through the latter part of 1888 and the following year, but it's not known if there was any connection to the Ripper killings. Jack the Ripper was the signature on one of many letters on the case sent to the police and the press, but it's far from certain it was from the killer. It may even have been written by a journalist to add to the story.

In the century that followed, more than a hundred names were added to the list of possible suspects. They included Albert Victor, Duke of Clarence and Avondale, the son of the future King Edward VII and grandson of Queen Victoria. Another alleged suspect was Henry Newbolt's artist friend, Walter Sickert. But the evidence against them and others is flimsy.

The adding of Thompson's name to the Ripper suspects list began in 1967 with the publication of John Walsh's biography *Strange Harp, Strange Symphony*. Walsh writes of a 'bizarre coincidence' between Thompson's search for his prostitute friend and the murders of five prostitutes, which Walsh said would have heightened Thompson's concern for her. He also suggests it is not beyond the realms of possibility that Thompson was questioned by police. He was after all a drug addict, acquainted with prostitutes and, most alarming, a former medical student.

This caught the attention of Dr Joseph Rupp, a forensic pathologist in Nueces County, Texas, who for the first time publicly raised the possibility that Thompson was the Ripper. Rupp laid out his case in an article in a British publication, the *Criminologist Magazine*, in 1988, the hundredth anniversary of the killings. He points to Thompson's drug addiction, his knowledge of the backstreets of London, his medical training, and the anger and violence of some of his poems. He concludes that it is just as likely that Thompson murdered his prostitute friend as that he went searching for her.

Rupp's article in turn inspired a full account of the case against Thompson by an Australian writer, Richard Patterson. In his 2017 book,

Jack the Ripper: The Works of Francis Thompson, Patterson recounts every aspect of Thompson's life and appears to find Ripper evidence in all of them. He goes back over Thompson's childhood, citing an incident when he demanded that his mother give him a doll like the ones his sisters had, then proceeded to cut its head open. He suggests that the anti-Catholic riots in Ashton-under-Lyne may have aggravated young Francis's troubled mind. And he argues that Thompson's years at medical school must have left him with dissecting skills, despite his alleged poor attendance record.

Patterson disputes the account by Everard Meynell of Thompson's break-up with his prostitute friend and offers what he admits is speculation about her departure, suggesting that he may have killed her or may have been driven by her departure into murdering others. He speculates that Wilfred Meynell, Thompson's protector, may have known that he was the Ripper and sent him off to a country monastery to protect him. He even suggests that Meynell senior had given Thompson the money to buy a new suit which would have made him more decent and attractive to the victims.

Some of the other evidence Patterson offers is also thin to the point of absurdity. He says that Dr Thomas Bond, the registered police surgeon for A Division, Westminster, wrote that the murderer must be in the habit of wearing a cloak or overcoat. Otherwise, he could hardly have escaped notice on the streets if the blood on his hands or clothes were visible. Patterson points out that Thompson was known for wearing a long overcoat in all weathers.

Arthur Conan Doyle, who took a break from the Sherlock Holmes stories to investigate the murders, told an American journalist that he thought the Ripper was 'a man accustomed to the use of a pen'. Patterson observes that Thompson knew how to use a pen. Perhaps the most chilling evidence Patterson offers is some of Thompson's own writings. They include a poem, unpublished at the time of the murders, entitled *Witch Babies*. It tells of a knight who kills a woman, a 'bedemon-ridden hag' and her two unborn children.

Thirteen more stanzas follow, including a particularly gruesome one:

Its paunch a-swollen,

Ha! Ha!

Its life a-swollen

Ho! Ho!

Like days drowned.

Harsh was its hum;

And its paunch was rent

Like a brasten drum;

And the blubbered fat

From its belly doth come

With a sickening ooze – Hell made it so!

Two witch-babies, ho! ho! ho!

Thompson undeniably had a seriously disturbed mind aggravated by drug addiction, and if a signed confession in his hand were to be belatedly discovered at the back of a desk drawer at Pantasaph, it would not be a complete surprise. But the evidence against him is wholly circumstantial. He was familiar with the streets of Whitechapel but so were hundreds of thousands of others. He did some dissecting at medical school but it's doubtful he had the expertise of the Ripper. At least Joseph Rupp acknowledged the uncertainty in his preface to Patterson's book: 'God bless you Francis Thompson and forgive you if I am right and God forgive me if I am wrong.'

Chapter 18

NEWBOLT AND
THE FOX HUNTER

IN HIS later years Newbolt found new friends among a younger generation of poets including Siegfried Sassoon and John Betjeman. Newbolt took to Sassoon because he was a good talker and a good cricketer. Sassoon saw Newbolt as a continuation of Victorianism.

Cricket played a much greater part in Sassoon's life than in Newbolt's, more even than in Francis Thompson's. He was born on 8 September 1886 to an Anglo-Catholic mother, Theresa, a daughter of the Thornycroft family of sculptors, and Alfred Ezra, the son of a wealthy Baghdadi Jewish family, the Sassoons. Alfred was cut off from the family after marrying outside the faith. Their son was called Siegfried not because of German roots, which he didn't have, but because his mother loved the music of Wagner.

When he was four, his parents split up, though his father visited Siegfried and his two brothers at weekends. The family lived at Matfield in the Weald of Kent and his cricket career began with the village XI. Years before, his father had played for the same team, umpired by a one-legged shoemaker, who later told the young Sassoon about his father's talents, 'A rare good one he was at getting his bat down to a shooter.'

Siegfried went on to play for the House at Marlborough School. By this time he was writing cricket poetry, though at this stage its gusto outweighed its subtlety. Even the titles were epic in length, *Dies Irae, (On Watching a Match in which Full Pitches by Fast Bowlers were among the Noticeable Points in the Game)* and *To Wilfred, Bowling, (A Reminiscence of the 2nd Test).*

He sent some poems to the school magazine, but they were not interested so he tried his luck with *Cricket, A Weekly Record of the Game*, edited by W.A. Bettesworth. There was controversy at the time about the height of the wicket, so Sassoon composed a parody of Charles Kingsley's *The Sands of Dee* and titled it *The Extra Inch*. Bettesworth liked the piece but regretted that he did not pay for poems. Sassoon did not complain. He said he would have paid Bettesworth to publish it.

O batsman, rise and go and stop the rot,

And go and stop the rot.

(It was indeed a rot,

Six down for twenty-three.)

The batsman thought how wretched was his lot.

And all alone went he.

The bowler bared his mighty, cunning arm

His vengeance – wreaking arm,

His large yet wily arm,

With fearful powers endowed,

The batsman took his guard. (A deadly calm

Had fallen on the crowd.)

O is it a half-volley or long-hop,

A seventh-bounce long-hop,

A fast and fierce long-hop,

That the bowler letteth fly?

The ball was straight and bowled him

    neck and crop.

He knew not how nor why.

Full sad and slow pavilionwards he walked.

The careless critics talked;

Some said that he was yorked;

A half-volley at a pinch.

The batsman murmured as he inward stalked,

'It was the extra inch.'

Away from school Sassoon played for the Bluemantle's club, based in Tunbridge Wells, occasionally turning out with Arthur Conan Doyle. The family's neighbours in Matfield included the Kent captain Frank Marchant and Sassoon had ambitions to play for his county but he didn't make the grade.

Three decades later, Sassoon recalled his village cricket days in his autobiographical novel, *Memoirs of a Fox-Hunting Man*. Renamed George Sherston, he arrives home from Marlborough on the train 'Ten minutes late, in the hot evening sunshine, my train bustled contentedly along between orchards and hop-gardens, jolted past the signal box, puffed importantly under the bridge, and slowed up at Baldock Wood.' He's met at the station by the family groom, Tom

Dixon. Like others in the story, Dixon also has an invented name. Even Matfield is renamed Butley.

Dixon tells him that they're both in the side for tomorrow's game, the Flower Show Match. Young George is thrilled. It's the fixture of the season, sharing the day with the village agricultural show. After a deep sleep he joins Dixon in the morning, and they white their pads with a tin of Blanco. He and his Aunt Evelyn (in real life his mother) walk to the cricket ground, where she will be judging the flower and vegetable show.

At noon, the opponents, Rotherden, arrive. Among them are two tall men with large drooping moustaches. Dixon points them out as the two demon fast bowlers, Crump and Bishop. Butley lose the toss and take to the field with the two umpires. The visiting official is Tom Seamark, a red-faced man 'as bulky as a lighthouse'. The home umpire is the one-legged man, Bill Sutler. No one knows how he lost his leg, but the neighbours believe he was fighting for Queen and Country. He's acknowledged to be biased in favour of his village team. After one controversial and match-deciding lbw decision, he is claimed to have been overheard reckoning, 'I've won my 5 bob.' He was also accused of making holes in the wicket with his wooden leg to help the Butley attack.

Crump and Bishop open for Rotherden. They both go cheaply but Rotherden make it to 183. The Butley brass band is playing *Soldier of the Queen* outside the horticultural tent, but it's drowned out by a steam organ booming out to accompany a roundabout with golden wooden horses. Eventually a Butley fielder orders the organ to stop and play is resumed. There is also trouble inside the horticulture tent. It has been discovered that the winner of the vegetable prize purchased his entry from another village's greengrocer.

Butley slowly near their target. George goes in at number ten and finds himself facing his first delivery needing one run to win with one wicket left. He nudges the ball away, scampers for a single and Butley are home.

The whole story is an idyllic picture of English village life which was to vanish a few years later. Sassoon had a simple view of world politics before the Great War, France was a lady, Russia was a bear, and turning out for the county side was much more important than either of them. But he joined the army as the conflict approached and by the time Britain declared war on Germany on 4 August 1914, he was serving with the Sussex Yeomanry. His arrival at the front was delayed by a broken arm from a riding accident. He finally arrived in France in November 1915, a few days after his younger brother Hamo died of injuries suffered in the Gallipoli campaign.

Sassoon was to display exceptional bravery. His exploits included the single-handed capture of a German trench, driving the enemy away with bombs. But he annoyed his commanding officer by sitting in the trench for two hours reading poetry instead of calling up support. In July 1916 he was awarded the Military Cross for spending an hour and a half under fire rescuing wounded comrades. There was no cricket, apart from the odd off-duty game with a stump for a bat, a wooden ball, and an old brazier as a wicket to bowl at.

But his anger at the horrors of the conflict was growing. In August 1916 he was shipped home to a makeshift hospital for officers at Somerville College, Oxford, suffering from gastric fever. He was joined there by his comrade and friend, the writer Robert Graves. Once recovered he refused to go back to the front and wrote a letter to his commanding officer entitled

'Finished with the war', arguing that while the war he had joined had been one of defence and liberation, it had now become a war of aggression and conquest. His 'Soldier's Declaration' was given to the press and read out in the Commons by a supportive MP.

He was risking court martial, but the government finally decided he should be sent to the Craiglockhart War Hospital in Edinburgh to be treated for neurasthenia, or shell shock, as suggested by Robert Graves. Here he began a close friendship with another war poet, Wilfred Owen. Sassoon encouraged Owen to write about life and death in the trenches and helped with two of his most famous poems, *Dulce et Decorum Est* and *Anthem for Doomed Youth*.

What passing-bells for these who die as cattle?
– Only the monstrous anger of the guns.
Only the stuttering rifles' rapid rattle

Can patter out their hasty orisons.

No mockeries now for them; no prayers nor bells;

Nor any voice of mourning save the choirs,

The shrill, demented choirs of wailing shells;

And bugles calling for them from sad shires.

What candles may be held to speed them all?

Not in the hands of boys, but in their eyes

Shall shine the holy glimmers of goodbyes.

The pallor of girls' brows shall be their pall;

Their flowers the tenderness of patient minds,

And each slow dusk a drawing-down of blinds.

Both men eventually decided their supreme responsibility was to the men serving under them and returned to active service in France. Sassoon was wounded again, this time by a British soldier who mistook him for a German. Sassoon spent the rest of the war back in Britain. Owen was killed a week before the Armistice.

Back home after the war, Sassoon became a giant of the literary scene, particularly the radical side. In his *Later Life* autobiographical work, Henry Newbolt recalls that Sassoon sent him a collection of poems by Wilfred Owen with an introduction by Sassoon himself. Newbolt found the poems 'terribly good' but limited. 'All one and the same note.' He thought that Owen and the broken men railed at the old men who sent the young to die; the young had suffered cruelly, but in the nerves and not the heart. He didn't think the shell-shocked war poems would move the generation's grandchildren.

After a number of relationships with men, Siegfried Sassoon married in 1933 and a son was born three years later. Throughout the post-war period, his passion for cricket remained. In his later years he played for the Downside Abbey team, the Ravens, and was still turning out in his seventies. Sassoon died of stomach cancer

on 1 September 1967, a week before his 81st
birthday.

Chapter 19

RETURN TO ORCHARDLEIGH

THROUGHOUT THE war Newbolt had maintained his view of its merits and glories. Now he had to face the loss of friends and the sons of friends and the trauma of Francis, who woke in the night screaming from dreams of war. In September 1920, father and son visited the battlefield at Ypres and Francis led him through the holed and devastated fields he had fought in. After Newbolt's death, a brief, unpublished poem was found among his papers. It was entitled *A Perpetual Memory: Good Friday, 1915.*

Broken and pierced, hung on the bitter wire,

By their most precious death the Sons of Man

Redeem for us the life of our desire—

O Christ how often since the world began!

Newbolt's war propaganda days were over but his social and professional contacts helped him into a new role. The president of the Board of Education, H.A.L. Fisher, asked him to chair a new committee planning the teaching of English in schools. Two years later his report was published to wide acclaim and was used in teacher training colleges until 1942.

Domestically, Newbolt's life was in some turmoil. In 1919 his mother, Emily, died after suffering a stroke. Frank upset Newbolt by announcing that he wished to marry Nancy Triffitt, a young art student who had lodged in the same house as him. Newbolt was not happy about the relationship, possibly because Nancy was too low on the social ladder, but he finally agreed. By the end of the 1920s Margaret was suffering from increasing deafness and finally travelled to a clinic in Freiburg for treatment. While she was being treated, Newbolt went off to the Alps with Ella.

Socially and professionally, Newbolt was still thriving. In 1922 he was made a Companion of Honour and the following January he went on a lecture tour of Canada at the invitation of the Canadian Council, travelling coast to coast with 81 stopping points. The audiences were enthusiastic, but Newbolt thought the only one of his poems they had heard of was *Play Up*. 'It's a kind of Frankenstein's Monster that I created thirty years ago and I now find it falling on my ears at every corner,' he noted.

At the end of the decade, he and Kipling were invited to lunch by Sir John Reith, director general of the recently formed BBC, to discuss a series of radio broadcasts. Kipling decided he was not learned enough but Newbolt went ahead. He also had the strange experience of returning to Bilston to unveil, while still alive, a memorial to himself in the form of a bronze plaque on the wall of St Mary's Church. He spent the night at the vicarage which he had left when he was three years old.

In 1933 Newbolt showed the first signs of the mysterious illness which was to end his life. He and Margaret decided to leave Netherhampton and they both moved into Ella's house on Camden Hill, Kensington, which was extended to accommodate them. Margaret and Ella were reunited at last. Newbolt's health continued to deteriorate, and he sank deep into himself. He died on 19 April 1938 aged 75 after suffering a stroke, and was buried in the churchyard of St Mary's on an island in the lake at Orchardleigh.

In 1940, at the height of the Battle of Britain, the young John Betjeman produced a collection of Newbolt's poems. His introduction read, 'He stood for the England of Empire Builders, country gentlemen, high moral Christian values, and English scenery. He was one of a generation which is passing but which is, with all its faults, loveable and honest.'

Chapter 20

SUPERFINE

On a small ground, in a small town

In Lancashire, a small man,

Ramadhin, is bowling; his arm comes over

Making disbelievers believe in magic.

Colin Shakespeare

FRANCIS THOMPSON'S immortalising of
Hornby and Barlow was echoed half a century
later, this time with words and music. David
Rayern Allen's 1981 collection *A Song For Cricket*
tells the story of cricket songs written for music
halls, clubs and jollies up to and through the

Victorian era. It includes verses written by J. Burnby in the 18th century and put to music for two tenors and bass by Samuel Porter in 1825:

What's the matter, my friends, at
   Sheffield to-day,
That most of the people are going away?
What's the matter, indeed! – why, don't you
   know, Mester,
That Nottingham's playing both Sheffield
   and Leicester.
Hey derry, derry down, etc.

In 1950 cricket music was back, in calypso form. A leading voice belonged to Egbert Moore, born in Port of Spain, Trinidad, in 1906. Renaming himself Lord Beginner, he grew up to be one of the island's great calypso musicians. In May 1934, an expatriate Portuguese businessman, Edward Sa Gomes, sent him off to New York with two

217

other calypsonians, Attila the Hun and Growling Tiger, to record for the Port of Spain label which helped spread calypso worldwide.

In July 1948, Lord Beginner had travelled to London with two other musicians, Lord Kitchener (Aldwyn Roberts), from Arima in Trinidad and Tobago, and Lord Woodbine (Harold Philips) from nearby Laventille. Lord Kitchener was to be the creator of cricket's greatest calypso, and Lord Beginner its recorded voice. They sailed on the *Empire Windrush* on the first of its many voyages carrying West Indians to Britain. By 1950, Lord Kitchener was a regular performer on BBC Radio and in live shows, and Lord Beginner was playing in clubs across London and recording for Parlophone, when the West Indies team arrived for their first tour of England since the end of World War Two.

Teams of English cricketers had been touring the West Indies since 1894, playing mostly

white teams, and in 1900 the white Trinidadian
Aucher Warner, brother of the future England
captain Pelham Warner, brought a side to
England, though it didn't have first-class status.
Tours on both continents continued until the
1920s. Finally in 1926 the West Indies, along
with India and New Zealand, joined England
(aka MCC), Australia and South Africa in the
Imperial Cricket Conference, clearing the way
for Test status.

The first West Indies Test tour of England in
1928 ended with a 3-0 victory for the home side,
with wins at Lord's, Old Trafford and the Oval.
West Indies were more successful in the first
series on home territory in 1929/30, drawing 1-1
with defeat at Queen's Park Oval, Port of Spain
and a win at Bourda in Georgetown, Guyana,
then British Guiana. There were also two draws.

This was to be the pattern for the next 20
years. West Indies took the next home series

in 1934/35 2-1, winning at Queen's Park Oval
and Sabina Park, Kingston, Jamaica. But right
through the next three decades they failed to win
a single Test on English soil. This was despite the
presence of two of the greatest names in cricket
history, George Headley and Learie Constantine.

George Alphonse Headley had a remarkable
record while propping up a moderate West Indies
side. His batting average was 60.83 in Test matches
and 69.86 in all first-class games. Headley was
born in Panama but grew up in Jamaica and made
his name playing for the Jamaican side. He just
missed selection for the 1928 England tour but
made his Test debut in 1930 in Barbados. After
the 1933 England tour he played club cricket for
Haslingden in the Lancashire League until war
broke out in 1939.

The great West Indian philosopher and cricket
writer, C.L.R. James, who played alongside
Headley in Lancashire, rated him second only

to Donald Bradman among the world's great batsmen, and that was a close-run thing. He points out that Headley usually had to hold the innings together himself, while Bradman had the support of Woodfull, Ponsford, McCabe, Kippax, Brown and Hassett. James reckons his greatest strength was seeing the ball early. Headley once told him he saw every ball bowled come out of the bowler's hand. If he missed it, he was in trouble.

After the war he was appointed West Indies captain against the England tourists in 1948, the first black player to hold the job, though he only played one game as skipper. After several seasons of league cricket in Lancashire and Birmingham, he returned to Jamaica, where he was appointed cricket coach by the government. He died in 1983. His son Ron played for the West Indies and his grandson Dean for England.

My late uncle Bob Travis once told me of an afternoon he spent as a young man watching

Nelson in the Lancashire League. At one point, when Nelson were in the field, an opposition batsman hit the ball high in the air. It dropped swiftly towards the head of a Nelson fielder. At the last split second the fielder leaned forward, cupped his hands behind him and caught the ball behind his back.

The fielder was Learie Nicholas Constantine, born in Trinidad and Tobago on 21 September 1901. C.L.R. James describes him as a great bowler and a great batsman, but above all a brilliant fielder. C.L.R., who lodged with him until Learie and Neville Cardus found him work for the *Manchester Guardian*, also thought he was a league cricketer who played Test cricket, not a Test cricketer who played in the leagues.

Cricket ran in Learie's family. His father, known as 'Cons', was a fine batsman. In 1900 he was selected to tour England, but as a non-professional without much money, he couldn't afford to go. In the end, after the team boat had left for England, he was spotted on the street, a public whip-round was held, and he was put on a fast launch to catch up with the team boat before it reached the high seas.

After a promising start to his own cricketing career at home, young Learie was picked for the West Indies side to tour England in 1923, and five years later he was back to take the West Indies' first wicket in Tests. Some of his performances on the tour were extraordinary. C.L.R. James recalls a match against Middlesex in which he went in to bat at 79/5. He scored 50 in 20 minutes and 86 in less than an hour. He then took six wickets for 11 in 6.1 overs. In the second innings he went in at 121/5 and scored 103 runs out of 133 in an hour, including 50 in 18 minutes. He played for Nelson between 1929 and 1938 while touring England and Australia for the West Indies.

In a remarkable career after the war, he served as Trinidad and Tobago's high commissioner to the United Kingdom and became the first black member of the House of Lords. He campaigned fiercely against racial discrimination, and served on the Race Relations Board, the Sports Council, and the Board of Governors of the BBC. Lord Constantine died on 1 July 1971.

By 1950, the West Indies batting line-up was strong, even without Headley and Constantine, thanks to the arrival of the three Ws, Clyde Walcott, Everton Weekes and Frank Worrell. The bowling was less promising, but two young players caught the eye of the skipper, John Goddard. Alf Valentine, who was 20, and 21-year-old Sonny Ramadhin had each played only two first-class matches, both against each other, Trinidad versus Jamaica. Ramadhin clinched his place in the touring side with 12 wickets in the two matches, becoming the first cricketer of Indian origin to play for the West Indies. Valentine took only two wickets in the two games, but Goddard saw some talent.

Alf Valentine was born in Spanish Town, 20 miles from Kingston, Jamaica, and worked as an apprentice machinist, finding time to practise bowling. He relied heavily on his tweaking finger and regularly carried a bottle of surgical spirit to treat it between spells.

Sonny Ramadhin was born in Esperance Village, Trinidad and Tobago. His parents were both descendants of indentured workers brought over from India and were employed on a sugar cane plantation. Sonny learned the game at the Canadian Mission School in Duncan village and polished his bowling accuracy while working on an estate farm. His job included work on the local cricket pitch and the club secretary called on Sonny and his pals to give him some batting practice. He put a penny on the stumps and gave it to anyone who bowled him. Nothing for caught or lbw.

In his history of spin bowling, *Twirlymen*, Amol Rajan sees Ramadhin and Valentine as two great but very different bowlers. Ramadhin was short, with a thin moustache, and described by Richie Benaud as 'basically an off-spinner with a deceptive leg-break'. Valentine was tall, lithe and bespectacled, a classic left-arm orthodox bowler.

Valentine did not impress in the opening games of the 1950 England tour and wasn't sure of his place in the side for the first Test. But in the final warm-up game, against Lancashire, he took 8-26 in the first innings and 5-41 in the second, leading the West Indies to victory by an innings and 220 runs.

On the opening morning of the first Test at Old Trafford, Valentine took five wickets before lunch, finishing with 8-104. He picked up three more wickets in the second innings, but England won the match by 202 runs. The second Test opened at Lord's on 24 June. Allan Rae, opening for the West Indies, made 106, and 63 by Weekes and 52 by Worrell took them to 326. Len Hutton and Cyril Washbrook started solidly for England, but Hutton was caught by Walcott off Valentine for 35 and Washbrook was stumped, again by Walcott, off Ramadhin for 36. England then fell apart, with Ramadhin taking 5-66 and Valentine 4-48. Only Johnny Wardle (33) and skipper Norman Yardley (16) reached double figures.

The West Indies built on their first-innings lead of 175 with a mighty 68 not out by Walcott, backed up by Gerry Gomez with 70 and Weekes with 63. Goddard declared at 425/6, setting England 601 to win with nearly two full days to go. By the close England still needed 383 runs to win with six wickers remaining. Washbrook had held the innings together and was 114, but on the final morning he was bowled by Ramadhin without adding to his score and at 2.18pm England were dismissed for 274, losing by 326 runs. Ramadhin finished with 6-43 in the second innings and Valentine 3-79. The crowd on the final day was small and fewer than a hundred were West Indian, but cricket writer Martin Williamson recalls on Cricinfo how they made a tremendous racket with drums and maracas and in one case a cheese grater and a carving knife. He also observes that BBC radio and television missed the drama because of *Women's Hour* and Wimbledon coverage.

When the last wicket fell the players sprinted to the pavilion carrying stumps as souvenirs. Thwarted from joining the players, the supporters circled the ground sharing rum, while MCC laid on champagne in the dressing rooms. Ramadhin, a teetotall who only ever drank ginger beer, did not stay long and had dinner with friends from Trinidad studying in London. Meanwhile, a band of West Indian fans sang and danced their way from Lord's to Piccadilly and around Eros.

Among the songs was a new number, *The Victory Calypso*, or *Cricket, Lovely Cricket*. It's unclear how the number evolved. One of the fans, Sam Cook, later the Mayor of Southwark, told *The Guardian* in 1998 that he was getting ready to go home when someone told him: 'You can't go home, Kitchener is going to make a song.' The gang sat down on the grass and Kitchener said 'Cricket, lovely cricket'. Martin Williamson reckons the final product was a team effort.

John Arlott called it the first truly bipartisan Test: 'Not only were the West Indian followers delighted, but English spectators, who had never known such a jolly atmosphere at cricket matches, were carried along by the carefree yet, at the same time, purposeful cricket of the tourists.'

England went on to win the third Test at Trent Bridge by ten wickets and the fourth at the Oval by an innings and 56 runs, taking the series 3-1. Valentine finished with a series total of 33 wickets and Ramadhin 26.

Meanwhile, Lord Beginner was recording *Cricket, Lovely Cricket* on the Melodisc label with the Calypso Rhythm Kings chiming in with *Ramadhin and Valentine*. The song came out of the wireless throughout the 1950s and was back on air in March 2022 when Sonny Ramadhin died.

The King was there well attired,
So they started with Rae and Stollmeyer;
Stolly was hitting balls around the boundary;
But Wardle stopped him at twenty.
Rae had confidence,
So he put up a strong defence;
He saw the King was waiting to see,
So he gave him a century.

Chorus: With those two little pals of mine

Ramadhin and Valentine.

West Indies first innings total was

   three-twenty-six

Just as usual

When Bedser bowled Christiani

The whole thing collapsed quite easily;

England then went on,

And made one-hundred-fifty-one;

West Indies then had two-twenty lead

And Goddard said, 'That's nice indeed.'

Chorus: With those two little pals of mine

Ramadhin and Valentine.

Yardley wasn't broken-hearted

When the second innings started;

Jenkins was like a target

Getting the first five in his basket.

But Gomez broke him down,

While Walcott licked them around;

He was not out for one-hundred and sixty-eight,

Leaving Yardley to contemplate.

Chorus: With those two little pals of mine

Ramadhin and Valentine.

West Indies was feeling homely,

Their audience had them happy.

When Washbrook's century had ended,

West Indies voices all blended.

Hats went in the air.

They jumped and shouted without fear;

So at Lord's was the scenery

Bound to go down in history.

Chorus: After all was said and done

Second Test and the West Indies won!

Ramadhin and Valentine's last Test series together against England was in 1957. It was a very frustrating tour, thanks largely to a controversial tactic deployed by two of England's top batsmen, the captain Peter May and Colin Cowdrey, in the first Test at Edgbaston. The two came together with England struggling at 113/3, chasing West Indies' 288. Their strategy was to place their left leg well down the track to nudge away the balls pitching outside the off stump without risking lbw. The West Indians thought it was as unsporting a tactic as Bodyline, but it saved England from the humiliation of 1950, and they won the series 3-0 with two draws.

Alf Valentine returned to the West Indies side for the tour of England in 1963 but was very much a back-up for Garfield Sobers and Lance Gibbs. He stayed in England to play in the Birmingham League for a few years. After the death of his first wife Gwendolyn, the mother of four daughters, he married his second wife, an American, Jaquelyn, and they moved to Great Oaks near Orlando, Florida.

Alf was a generous-hearted man. After matches he would stay behind signing autographs, sometimes with Ramadhin, long after their team-mates had gone. In Great Oaks, he and Jacquelyn acted as substitute parents looking after abused or abandoned children whose parents were in prison. Alf died on 11 May 2004, aged 74.

After his Test career was over, Sonny Ramadhin followed in the footsteps of Hornby and Barlow, playing for Lancashire in 1964 and 1965, until he decided he was past his best and ended his contract. From 1968 to 1972 he played for Lincolnshire in the Minor Counties Championship, before moving to the Lancashire League, turning out for Crompton, Radcliffe, Little Lever, and Daisy Hill, as well as teams in Huddersfield, North Staffordshire and South Cheshire.

With his wife June he settled in Saddleworth where for over 30 years he was licensee of the Hare and Hounds and the Cloggers Arms in Uppermill and the White Lion, Delph. His grandson Kyle Hogg played for Lancashire from 2001–14. As late as early 2022 the *Saddleworth Independent* reported that, aged 92, Sonny was attending every game at Friarmere where his son Craig had played for 50 seasons. Sonny died a few days later on 27 February 2022, outliving Alf by 17 years. He was 92.

Back in 1995, in his poetry collection *Seamers*, the Yorkshire-born writer Colin Shakespeare recalled Ramadhin in the local leagues:

Time was he could make cities move,

Crowds converged, with applause ringed him;

Magic enough, his shirt sleeve flapping,

England, no wicket could read him.

Hutton said, 'Treat him like a great man,

Play him down the line.'

Play him down the line into

The passages of time.

Chapter 21

LEGACIES

IN AN early scene in *Private's Progress*, the Boulting Brothers' wartime satire made in 1956, a military bigwig addresses a squad of recruits from the University Training Corps, preparing to enter the fight against Hitler's Germany. He tells the newcomers, including, as always, Ian Carmichael and Richard Attenborough, 'We British are a peace-loving people. Our national game is cricket.

'We expect fair play, we stick to the rules, and our sympathies are always with the underdog, the little chap.'

However, 'The enemy does not play cricket. He abides by no rules whatsoever. I can tell you, there is no kind of frightfulness he won't impart. What we have to do therefore, is to show the enemy that when it comes to frightfulness, we can be pretty frightful ourselves.'

This is a gentle parody of the view of cricketing fair play set out in *Vitai Lampada*: Batsmen, walk if you're caught behind and know you got an edge; bowlers, don't aim to hit the batsman on the head. But Newbolt goes beyond the cricket field and on to the battlefield, eliciting devotion, anger and some amusement in the century and more since it was written.

This is the word that year by year,

While in her place the school is set,

Every one of her sons must hear,

And none that hears it dare forget.

This they all with a joyful mind

Bear through life like a torch in flame,

And falling fling to the host behind – 'Play up!

   play up! and play the game!'

Newbolt summed up his view of war when translating from *Chronicles of Froissart*, written by the 14th-century author Jean Froissart, who was born in the Low Countries. 'I hope my Froissart may do something for Chivalry which would be more useful than all the Peace Societies in the world, for men must always fight, the only difference being how they do it.'

But while fair play on the cricket field may be an indisputable treasure, the idea that fair play can be applied to killing one's enemies became more questionable, particularly after the horrors of the First World War, when a new generation of poets, like Wilfred Owen, saw the slaughter at first hand. He said, 'I am not concerned with Poetry. My subject is War, and the pity of War.

The Poetry is in the pity.' And *Vitai Lampada*'s imperialist strain sounded less comfortable as the Empire broke away. The author Sean French complained 30 years ago about 'Newbolt's fatuous equation of public-school cricket with the quelling of natives at the far reaches of the Empire.'

But in 1940, during the Battle of Britain, English-speaking countries such as Canada turned again to Newbolt's lines. In October that year, the *Montreal Gazette* told its readers of the damage done to English public schools by the Blitz and recalled the closing stanza of *Vitai Lampada*. But it declared it was not only the boys of the select schools who were carrying the torch. 'The King and Queen are holding it aloft, as are the humblest of their subjects, some of whom have had very little schooling. They are Britons all, united as never before by common danger. All are playing the game, and the torch they bear represents freedom. As such it is a far more powerful incentive to patriotism than is the Nazi swastika.'

As for cricket, long before Bodyline, sledging and ball-tampering, Dr Grace was refusing to walk and telling the umpire, 'They came to see me, not you.' But Newbolt's verses remained a torch for what E.W. Swanton described as 'a game which is reasonable, skilful, carried out with the participants' full industry and effort, frequently epic, aesthetically pleasing, and native to the English soil and people'.

Newbolt's sporting legacy went beyond England and beyond cricket. Grantland Rice was born in Tennessee in 1880 and was the son of a cotton dealer who became one of the most famous sports journalists in America. In 1941 he published a poem entitled *Alumnus Football*. Like *Vitai Lampada*, it begins in a sporting arena, in this case a college football field. It ends with a verse that Newbolt could have written.

For when the One Great Scorer comes to write

    against your name,

He marks – not that you won or lost – but how

    you played the game.

Readers of Francis Thompson fall into two distinct camps. Studies and collections of his work rarely mention *At Lord's*. Cricket enthusiasts treasure it but usually know little or nothing of his other work, except, occasionally, *The Hound of Heaven*. In contrast to *Vitai Lampada*, *At Lord's* is not about cricket and war; it's about cricket, memory and mortality. Thompson writes as a dying man recalling the cricketers of his youth with a mixture of joy and regret. And Thompson immortalised Hornby and Barlow in a way unequalled until Lord Beginner and Lord Kitchener rhapsodised the two great West Indian spinners.

    Sonny and Alf bowling at Monkey and Dick? Now that's a picture.

ACKNOWLEDGEMENTS

I USED to picture all authors sitting in self-imposed solitary confinement, taking the occasional break to put the kettle on. More recently I have learned how one relies on the support of friends and the generous advice of experts.

First of all, my thanks go to my wife, Martha, for her loving support, advice and patience, even though baseball, not cricket, is her national game; to my friend and neighbour Charles Walker for his guidance through the world of publishing; and of course, to Mihir Bose for his splendid foreword.

I'm grateful also to a long list of friends from school days, work, cricket and life: Paul Lakeland, Tom Walsh, Jonathan Baker, Tom Fort, Phil Harding, Marcy Leavitt Bourne, David Boardman, Khame Persaud, Ted Dougherty, Maurice Sukul, Paul Beard, Ausbert Scoon, Mike Barnes, Michael Glover, Richard Evans, Teddy Levitt Bourne, Fran Acheson and Sue Richards.

My warmest thanks to John Shakespeare, who, with the support of his mother, allowed inclusion of the moving poem on Sonny Ramadhin by his late father, Colin Shakespeare.

My thanks also to Roland John of Hippopotamus Press for approving the inclusion of *History* by Humphrey Clucas.

Three generous providers of photographs from cricket's history also shared valuable knowledge and advice on the game's story. Dr C.S. Knighton gave guidance on Clifton College. Malcolm Lorimer advised on Lancashire cricket and Francis Thompson; and Alan Rees provided a feast from MCC's picture library.

Thanks to *Wisden* for agreeing to the use of pictures of scorecards from two of the great matches.

I'm deeply indebted to the British Library and the team who helped my research with knowledge and patience, and I greatly appreciate the help of the Society of Authors, especially on issues of copyright.

And my warmest thanks, of course, to all at Pitch Publishing: Jane Camillin, Bruce Talbot, Dean Rockett, Duncan Olner, Graham Hales and all the team.

Humphrey Clucas, *History* from *Unfashionable Songs*, first published by Hippopotamus Press, 1991.

John Masefield, excerpt from *Eighty Five to Win*, included by permission of the Society of Authors as the literary representatives of the estate of John Masefield.

Walter de la Mare, permission to include four lines from *The Listeners* kindly agreed by the Literary Trustees of Walter de la Mare and the Society of Authors as their representative.

Siegfried Sassoon, *The Extra Inch* and *The Blues at Lord's* included by kind permission of the estate of George Sassoon.

BIBLIOGRAPHY

Adams, Roger, *Famous Writers on Cricket* (Partridge Press, 1988).

Arlott, John, *My Favourite Cricket Stories* (Readers Union Group of Book Clubs, 1976. First published by Butterworth Press, 1974).

Bearshaw, Brian, *From the Stretford End, The Official History of Lancashire CCC* (London: Transworld Publishers, 1989).

Beldam, G.W.., and Fry, C.B. *Great Batsmen, Their Methods at a Glance* (Macmillan & Co., 1907).

Bose, Mihir, *The Nine Waves – How India Took Over the Cricket World* (Pitch Publishing, 2022).

Butter, Peter, *Francis Thompson* (London: Longmans, Green and Co, for British Council and The National Book League, 1961).

Clucas, Humphrey, *Unfashionable Songs* (Hippopotamus Press, 1991).

Chitty, Susan, *Playing the Game – A Biography of Sir Henry Newbolt* (London: Quartet Books, 1997).

Fay, Stephen and Kynaston, David, *Arlott, Swanton and the Soul of English Cricket* (Bloomsbury Publishing, 2018).

Galsworthy, John, *The Forsyte Saga, the White Monkey* (William Heinemann, 1924. Paperback publication by Headline, 2007).

Hammond, N.G.L., *Centenary Essays on Clifton College* (1962).

Hardcastle, Graham and Ostick, Chris, *Champions ... About Blooming Time* (Nantwich: Max Books in association with Lancashire CCC, 2011).

Hayes, Dean, *Lancashire CCC Stadia* (Stroud: Tempus Publishing, 2007).

James, C.L.R., *Beyond a Boundary* (London: Stanley Paul & Co., 1963; Copyright Estate of C.L.R. James).

James, C.L.R., *A Majestic Innings – Writings on Cricket* (London: Aurum Press, 2006; first published by Allison & Busby, 1986).

Keigwin, R.P., *Public Schools Cricket 1901–1950* (Editor W.N. Roe, 1962).

Mailey, Arthur, *Opposing My Hero, From 10 for 66 and All That* (J.M. Dent & Sons, 1958).

Major, Sir John, *More Than a Game – The Story of Cricket's Early Years* (London: Harper Press, an imprint of Harper Collins, 2007).

Meynell, Everard, *The Life of Francis Thompson* (Burns & Oates, 1913; republished by Alfa Editions, 2018).

Newbolt, Henry, *The Twymans – A Tale of Youth* (William Blackwood, 1911).

Patterson, Richard, *Jack the Ripper: The Works of Francis Thompson* (London: Austin Macauley Press, 2017).

Rayvern Allen, David & Doggart, Hubert, *A Breathless Hush – The MCC Anthology of Cricket Verse* (London: Methuen, 2007).

Rayvern Allen, David, *A Song for Cricket* (London: Pelham Books, 1981).

Rajan, Amol, *Twirlymen* (London: Yellow Jersey Press, 2011).

Sassoon, Siegfried, *Memoirs of a Fox-Hunting Man* (London: Faber & Faber, 1928).

Sassoon, Siegfried, *The Old Century,* (London: Faber & Faber, 1938).

Shakespeare, Colin, *Seamers* (Bradford Oak Press, 1983).

Shenton, Kenneth, *O My Hornby and My Barlow Long Ago* (Nantwich: Max Books, 2019).

Taylor, Beverly, *Francis Thompson* (Boston, Mass: Twayne Publishers, 1987).

Telfer, Kevin, *Peter Pan's First XI* (London: Hodder & Stoughton, London, 2010).

Thompson, Francis, *Essays of Today and Yesterday* (George Harrap & Co., 1927).

Thompson, Francis, *Poems – 9th Edition* (London: Burns & Oates, 1908).

Thompson, Francis, *Collected Poems of* (Hodder & Stoughton, 1913).

Thompson, Francis, *Selected Poems – Burns, Oates and Washbourne* (Miami: Hard Press Publishing).

Walsh, John, *Strange Harp, Strange Symphony – The Life of Francis Thompson* (London: W.H. Allen, 1967).

Wynne-Thomas, Peter with Statham, Brian, *The History of Lancashire CCC* (London: Christopher Helm, 1989).

WEBSITES CONSULTED

https://en.wikipedia.org/wiki/Henry_Newbolt
(Henry Newbolt)

https://arcspace-pub.lib.cam.ac.uk/agents/
people/13924 (Laura Coltman/ Newbolt)

https://www.casebook.org/suspects/ft.html
(Francis Thompson / Ripper /Richard

Patterson)

https://www.casebook.org/ripper_media/book_
reviews/non-fiction/cjmorley/186.html

Francis Thompson / Ripper)

https://en.wikipedia.org/wiki/Clifton_College
(Clifton College)

https://en.wikipedia.org/wiki/Lord's
(Lord's History)

https://www.espncricinfo.com/story/those-two-
little-pals-of-mine-251196 (Victory Calypso)

https://singhiv.wordpress.com/2015/08/29/k-s-
ranjitsinhji-batting-wizard-destined-to-be-

king-excerpt-from-indra-vikram-singhs-book-dons-century/ (Ranjitsinhji)

https://en.wikipedia.org/wiki/List_of_William_McGonagall_poems (William McGonagall)

https://www.poetryfoundation.org/poets/siegfried-

sassoon#:~:text=Following%20the%20 outbreak%20of%20the,wounded%20 soldier%20d

uring%20heavy%20fire (Siegfried Sassoon)

https://warpoets.org/conflicts/great-war/siegfried-sassoon-1886-1967/ (Siegfried Sassoon)

https://en.wikipedia.org/wiki/Battle_of_Abu_Klea (Abu Klea)

https://www.arthur-conan-doyle.com/index.php/W._G._Grace:_A_Memory (Arthur Conan Doyle . W.G. Grace)

/https://en.wikipedia.org/wiki/Pranav_Dhanawade (Pranav Dhanawade)

https://www.panmacmillan.com/blogs/literary/
the-poetry-of-the-first-world-war (First
World War Poetry)

https://en.wikipedia.org/wiki/Lancashire_
County_Cricket_Club (Lancashire
County Cricket)

ABOUT THE AUTHOR

Bob Doran first played cricket on the green at Walton-le-Dale across the River Ribble from Preston in Lancashire. He studied classics at King's College, London, and joined the BBC as a trainee journalist working mostly in radio. He writes on cricket, classics and travel. He bowls off spin and fields in the gully. His batting position has slipped over the years from one to 11.